P9-CQM-267

CHiLDREN'S MiNiStRY
that Works!

revised and updated

The Basics and Beyond

CRAiG JutiLA . JiM WiDeMAN . CHRiS YOUNt
tHOM & JOANi SCHULtz . SUe MiLLeR . PAt VeRBAL
MARY RiCe HOPKiNS AND OtHeRS...

Group
Loveland, Colorado

CHILDREN'S MINISTRY THAT WORKS!

(revised and updated)

Copyright © 2002 by Group Publishing, Inc.
except "How to Make Changes in Your Children's Ministry"
© Sue Miller

Visit our Web site: **www.grouppublishing.com**

Credits

Editor: Mikal Keefer
Chief Creative Officer: Joani Schultz
Copy Editor: Lyndsay E. Gerwing
Book Designer: Jean Bruns
Computer Graphic Artist: Tracy K. Donaldson
Cover Art Director: Jeff A. Storm
Cover Designer: Blukazoo Studio
Cover Photographer: Daniel Treat
Production Manager: DeAnne Lear

Unless otherwise noted, Scripture taken from the HOLY
BIBLE, NEW INTERNATIONAL VERSION®. Copyright ©
1973, 1978, 1984 by International Bible Society. Used by permission of Zondervan Publishing House. All rights reserved.

Library of Congress Cataloging-in-Publication Data
Children's ministry that works!
     p. cm.
Includes bibliographical references.
  ISBN 0-7644-2407-6 (pbk. : alk. paper)
  1. Church work with children. 2. Christian education of
children. I. Group Publishing.
  BV639.C4 C44 2002
  259'.22--dc21
                                        2002003976

10 9 8 7 6 5 4 3 2 1   11 10 09 08 07 06 05 04 03 02
Printed in the United States of America.

contents

103867

CHILDREN'S MINISTRY THAT WORKS!

part 1

Children's Ministry Foundations

one

Setting a Vision, Staying the Course

by Christine Yount

To read most business books, creating and communicating a vision for your organization is no big deal.

You write a catchy statement, make a motivational speech, nail a plaque up on the cafeteria wall, and suddenly everyone understands where the organization is headed and how to get there. Costs drop, morale soars, and life is good.

If only it were that simple.

As many businesses have discovered, crafting and communicating a vision statement (these are sometimes called "mission statements") is a considerable challenge. It takes careful thought and an investment of time. And it's absolutely worth the effort.

Our children's ministries aren't businesses, but we must be every bit as strategic and focused as a for-profit corporation. We need to know where we're going and communicate that vision to every person serving in our ministry.

The Value of Vision

Dwight Mix, children's pastor at Fellowship Bible Church in Lowell, Arkansas, says, "Ministry, and a heart for ministry, travels the road of relationships. That means I have to help my staff see the vision and catch its passion by spending time with them. Then they in turn do the same with volunteers."

If relationships are the road for passing on a heart for ministry, vision is the fuel. What is it God is calling you to do in your children's ministry? A dynamic VBS outreach? A commitment to family-oriented programming? A thriving nursery ministry? To effectively lead volunteers, you must have a vision for what God wants. That vision, dream, or goal is best communicated in a vision statement.

Vision is "an element of ministry that can really add to and direct programs and ministry as a whole," says Carmen Kamrath, who has served as children's ministries director at Community Church of Joy in Glendale, Arizona. "First, pray about God's direction for your ministry. Second, talk to people about your vision statement before making it concrete; it helps to get others' views and to keep in mind the people you serve."

If drafting a vision statement sounds like a monumental task, then you understand what's at stake. It *is* a big deal. The document you draft will guide every ministry decision you make for months or even years to come.

But consider the alternative: Do you want to go through the next few months or years of ministry *without* the direction and clarity a vision statement brings?

Developing a Vision Statement for Your Ministry

As you draft your statement, consider these three areas: mission, method, and measure. Keep a pad of paper handy so that you can jot down notes and relevant Scriptures as you think about these issues.

• **Mission:** This part of your vision statement conveys your passion. What does God want your children's ministry to accomplish? What has God called your church to? Based on biblical imperatives, what do you believe God is calling your volunteer team to achieve with children?

Think big! Don't limit yourself to a puny reason for ministry—volunteers don't want to invest their lives in something that doesn't matter. But most people are captivated by a compelling, larger-than-life reason for reaching children.

According to Scripture, God's mission is to redeem or buy back the world through his Son, Jesus Christ. Second Corinthians 5:19 says, "God was reconciling the world to himself in Christ, not counting men's sins against them." Colossians 1:19-20 says, "God was pleased to have all his fullness dwell in him, and through him to reconcile to himself all things, whether things on earth or things in heaven, by making peace through his blood, shed on the cross."

As you consider what God is calling you to in your children's ministry, surround everything you do with the overarching biblical imperatives that you've received from God's Word. And what can be more compelling than affecting children's eternal destiny?

• **Method:** This is the big "how" question of your vision statement. How do you plan to do all that you have a vision for? What is God's plan for reaching your corner of the world? Your vision statement needs to contain the method you intend to employ.

Don't get into a detailed listing of programs here. Your goal is to identify an *approach* to Christian education that your program will embrace. Do you want to partner with families and support parents as the primary faith-shapers of their children? Do you believe Christian education is best delivered in classrooms? Are servant opportunities important to you?

• **Measure:** How will you know if you've realized your vision statement? Having specific measures in place helps build a sense of accomplishment as your volunteers see specific ways in which they're hitting the mark. And if you have a measure in place to know when you've accomplished your vision statement, you'll be able to celebrate with your team. Think about the end product you're trying to achieve. Whatever it is, that's what you should jot down as your measure.

The Vision Statement Temptation

You may be tempted to simply adopt the vision statement of another, successful ministry. Why not? After all, it's working for them.

Don't do it.

The process of creating your own vision statement is as valuable as the actual statement you create. Creating your own vision statement forces you to pull together key children's ministry leaders and prayerfully ask God what he wants to do through you. You'll hammer through the process of reaching a consensus. You'll discover, perhaps, that you've all had a different definition of what a successful ministry looks like.

An example: Several years ago a Sunday school teacher deliberately created small groups in his class so that kids could more easily debrief and apply the Bible lessons. It took months before the children actually opened up and believed it was acceptable to talk about their lives.

Before he left town on a four-week business trip, this teacher met with the substitute who'd be covering his class. The substitute nodded agreeably about the methodology he described and promised to carefully present the lessons he'd prepared in advance.

A month later he returned to find his classroom transformed. Chairs and a table filled the open space he'd used for discussion circles. Carefully lettered pieces of cardboard, each with the name of a book in the Bible, lined the walls. And half the kids were missing.

The substitute had discovered that not all the children could recite the books of the Bible in order and believed that was one solid measure of success for any Christian education program. So she set about fixing the omission.

Questioned about what had happened, she firmly announced that she'd "rescued" the children from biblical illiteracy—and she'd do the same thing again.

Who was right? Who was wrong?

An even better question: How could two such divergent views of what effective ministry to children looks like exist in one Christian education department?

Answer: There was no shared vision statement.

Asked to describe what a successful ministry looks like, how closely do the visions of *your* volunteers line up?

Don't just guess at how unified your team's vision might be. Check it out by pulling together key leaders and creating a vision statement that incorporates mission, method, and measurement. A word to the wise: This won't be a quick thing—or an easy one. You'll need to set aside several meetings. A suggested process follows:

Begin by creating a rough draft that does a pretty good job of summing up what people agree makes sense, given what Scripture says and what you know about your church and community. Work toward consensus in wording for each area.

Once your group completes a rough draft, ask, "Is this really what we're all about?" Then, working together, edit the statement.

Pick apart every word.

After editing, you're ready to critique what you've written by asking, "Why?" Form pairs and designate a reader and writer in each pair. Have the reader read a phrase of the vision statement. Then have the writer ask, "Why?" As the writer takes notes, the reader must respond with an answer. Continue this process until the entire statement is read. Then have pairs switch roles and do it again.

Bring pairs back together and ask:

- **What did you learn about our vision statement as you did this process?**
- **Are there any gaps in our vision statement? Explain.**
- **What things—if any—do we need to add to our vision statement?**
- **What things do we need to delete from our vision statement?**

If any significant issues arise, revisit your statement and re-edit. Then pare it down to the bare bones, using as few words as possible while still retaining the meaning.

Did you survive the process? Congratulations—you have a vision statement that key volunteers embrace and that will guide your ministry. Now it's time to communicate it to others!

---

*t*he Lake Pointe Baptist Church in Rockwall, Texas, created the following vision statement: "Partnering with families to reach and teach children in such a way that they have the greatest opportunity to become fully developing followers of Christ."

Imbedded in this vision statement is a *mission* volunteers can get excited about—it's compelling! Volunteers know that if they sign on for children's ministry, they'll be doing significant, life-changing ministry in children's lives.

The *method* is clearly spelled out too: "partnering with families." Parents will be welcomed and involved. There's a recognition that →

strengthening the homes of children matters.

And the *measure* is addressed. This ministry is committed to creating "fully developing followers of Christ." When children make conscious decisions to include spiritual disciplines in their lives and apply the Bible truths learned on Sunday throughout the week, then the children's ministry is doing something right. There's cause for celebration and praising God.

Vision Casting

Now that you and your leaders know where you're going, you want everyone involved in your ministry to have complete, passionate, to-die-for ownership of your mission. How do you accomplish this?

1. Memorize your vision statement. And not just you. Have your ministry leaders memorize it too. You want your team to be able to articulate the vision whenever a parent or potential volunteer inquires about your ministry.

2. Set goals according to your vision statement. Here's where the time you invested making sure your vision statement was on target pays off. Once you have a clear vision statement, it's easier for you and your staff to focus on what practical steps will help you fulfill it.

3. Broadcast your vision statement. Put it everywhere—on flyers, posters, business cards, stationery.

4. Partner with your pastor. Make sure your senior pastor has a copy of your vision statement. (You did remember to do this *before* you broadcast it to everyone else in your church, right?) If you can make a raving fan out of your pastor, communicating your vision to your volunteers will become much easier. Remember that senior pastors *hate* surprises. Plus, it's their responsibility to seek

God's vision for your church. It's your job to get a grasp of that vision and see how your ministry can support and flesh it out. Be sure you can explain how your ministry vision supports the pastor's larger vision for the church.

5. Call people to the vision, not the program. If you ask, "Would you like to teach the third-grade Sunday school class?" that's calling someone to a role. Instead, you want to ask a question that ties the volunteer into your vision, such as "Would you like to partner with parents of our third-graders to help these children become fully developing followers of Christ?" See the difference? The second question calls a volunteer to the big picture.

6. Train your volunteers in your vision statement. Talk about it. Talk about what it means. Ask your volunteers how they can embrace and implement it. And check back to see how you're doing compared to the measure that you determined was your mark of success.

7. Use your vision statement as a filter for decisions. Don't just file your vision statement under "V." Keep it at the forefront of your mind. Use it to make sound judgments that'll keep your ministry focused on what God has called you to do. Run every program, suggestion, brainstormed tweak, and Latest New Thing you hear trumpeted by a convention speaker through your vision statement. Does it help you fulfill the vision you've prayerfully, thoughtfully, created—or not?

If so, move ahead.

If not, no matter how good an idea it might be, decline.

What if You Have a Vision—and Everyone Else Is Wearing Blinders?

You're not alone. Moses had a vision of the Promised Land and went wherever God prompted him to get there. He was committed and focused.

But there were some who preferred to drag their feet out in the wilderness, more concerned with their current discomforts than with the larger vision of where they were going.

What can you do with feet-dragging volunteers?

First, cry out to God. That's what Moses did when he was in the wilderness—more than once. In Exodus 17:4, when the Israelites complained that they had no water, Moses was frustrated to the point of crying out, "What am I to do with these people? They are almost ready to stone me."

But they didn't. (And your volunteers probably won't, either.) When Moses cried out to God, the Lord answered and provided for the people's needs. Sometimes we just need to set our plans and schedules aside and wait on the Lord. Psalm 27:14 says, "Wait for the Lord; be strong and take heart and wait for the Lord." And Proverbs 20:22b says, "Wait for the Lord, and he will deliver you."

You have to know the threshold for change in your church and in your children's ministry. So many things can impact that threshold: the culture, the church's recent history, the economy, the changing membership or neighborhood, loyalties to past programming and curriculum. The list is nearly endless.

Move slowly as you determine where you are in terms of change. And don't push—you'll only alienate the very people whose hearts have to be changed to help you. See Chapter 6: How to Make Changes in Your Children's Ministry (pp. 71-81) for more detailed suggestions about how to proceed.

Realize that a new or freshly embraced vision may not be equally well received by all your existing volunteers. You can expect some resistance, and your timing for implementation may not be God's timing for making changes. Your willingness to prayerfully wait may be the strong testimony to your "foot draggers" that helps them feel less threatened. Your willingness to not simply declare, "My way or the highway!" may build trust that won't be built any other way.

Just be sure that as you wait, you keep talking about the vision God has given you for your ministry.

(This chapter is excerpted from Awesome Volunteers. Copyright © 1998 Christine Yount. Published by Group Publishing, Inc. For more practical tips and a solid methodology for finding—and keeping—volunteers, ask for this book at your local Christian bookstore or call Group at 1-800-447-1070.)

two

Determining and Developing Your Leadership Team

TAKING VOLUNTEER RECRUITMENT AND RETENTION TO THE NEXT LEVEL

by Craig Jutila

OK, let me admit it right up front: I was dragged into children's ministry kicking and screaming. I didn't even *like* children.

I wanted to do youth ministry, but when an executive pastor told me I *would* do children's ministry, I agreed—reluctantly. So reluctantly, in fact, that I wanted to put a time limit on the assignment.

But during those few years, God massaged my heart and let me see how my spiritual gifts, personality, and experience had shaped me for this ministry. Somewhere along the line, I realized I wasn't stuck in children's ministry; I *wanted* to be there.

Doing children's ministry is a blast, and one of the best

parts is working with the volunteers God has brought to Saddleback Church.

Keep in mind that we don't call them "volunteers." We call them "leaders" because that's what they are. They lead kids through their words and example.

Great teams of children's ministry leaders seldom come together on their own. It takes some leadership on your part, and we've been learning a lot about that at Saddleback the past few years.

I'd like to share what we're learning so that you can benefit from it too.

How to Get the Right People on Your Team

IT'S ABOUT COMPETENCY.

A few years ago, I put together a church hockey team. When I went to the rink to register, the gentleman working the counter asked, "Is your team bronze, silver, or gold?"

I had no idea what he was talking about.

He graciously explained that a bronze team plays at a beginner level and a gold team plays at tournament cup level. He wanted to know the skill level of our team. I asked him if there was a plastic league.

We started in the bronze league and had a great time. Over the next few years, we moved up in the league because the skill level of each player increased over time. As each player got better, our team as a whole got better.

When you form a leadership team, you ask all sort of questions: commitment questions, getting-to-know-you questions, how-long-have-you-been-a-believer questions. They're necessary questions, but if you want to play at the gold level, you have to assess *skill*.

Here's what I've discovered: You cannot train everybody for children's ministry. There are people who simply don't have the basic skills or temperament they need to be effective and other people who simply don't want to learn.

And the fact that a potential leader has taught before in another program somewhere doesn't mean much. Maybe that person taught *badly* back at his or her former church.

You need people who are *competent*. They have skills that can be sharpened, and they're willing to grow in their ministry skills.

Ask potential leaders to tell you about times they felt that they really connected with kids. How did they do it? What sort of lessons do they enjoy teaching? How do their philosophies of Christian education line up with your ministry's philosophy? Ask questions about how they'd handle specific discipline situations. What skills do you see? What skills do you *need* to see? Are you involving people who can actually do the tasks that need to be done?

IT'S ABOUT COMMITMENT.

If you want a gold-level ministry team, it's going to take work. Be honest with potential leaders about that right up front.

My leaders are required to attend four ministry enrichment sessions per year. They come, too, because the training not only helps them be better children's ministry leaders, but also more successful in life. When we teach about ministry time-management and leadership skills, that information is transferable to the workplace and home.

You're looking for leaders who *want* to serve and are willing to grow in their abilities as servants in children's ministry. That's going to require time and effort.

Here's a tip for getting new leaders to stick: Start small.

At Saddleback Church, we first invite potential leaders to do gateway commitments (small task-oriented projects that require little or no equipping). Once new leaders experience how great it is to minister to children, they usually come back for a little more responsibility. The key is to *never let them walk away discouraged.*

Here's an example of how we do it.

During the summer we have a weeklong "Summer Spectacular." It's our version of VBS, and during that time we'll bring fifty to one hundred new leaders on board to staff it. They go through the same background checks and fingerprinting we require of weekly volunteers, so they've cleared that hurdle.

After Summer Spectacular is over, we host a coffee for new leaders who helped with each age group. If there were ten new leaders working with fifth graders, we'll have all ten of them get together at someone's house.

We ask them how they liked the week and whether or not they felt they had an influence in the lives of some kids. We invite them to share a story about something that happened. We ask if they can see themselves doing ministry with fifth graders on a monthly basis, or a weekly basis.

When we get a "yes" on small things, we don't stop there—and neither should you. Expect your leaders to move ahead to the next level of service. Many will want to go there.

IT'S ABOUT CONSISTENCY.

If a leader is going to come in contact with a child, I want that person to be involved every week. If the leader can only give time every other week, fine—there are ministry opportunities that person can do too.

But if the leader is in contact with kids, it's every week. Period.

It's a matter of doing what's best for the kids we serve. Who's more effective in classrooms dealing with children: someone who rotates through a classroom once a month, or the leader who's there week after week? the person who walks through the door to share information, or the leader who knows children well enough to share life?

The Holy Spirit can use either leader, and we expect every leader to share accurate, biblical information. For sheer impact, the leader who's invested in the kids will win every time.

Consider the numbers: If Nancy serves once a month, that's approximately twelve hours per year she's with kids. If Beth serves every week, that's approximately fifty-two hours per year. On average, Beth sees the children in class four times more than the monthly teacher. That's forty extra opportunities to build relationships, increase community, and communicate a different and deeper type of care!

I know it's a common practice to recruit tons of leaders so that nobody has to be with the kids more than a few times per month, but is that approach the best way to encourage your kids to grow spiritually? Won't your kids be better served if they have a significant adult with whom they're comfortable opening up to talk?

Remember that you're not just recruiting teachers, you're also developing leaders. Build in time for those mentoring relationships to develop.

IT'S ABOUT CHEMISTRY.

This is about how a leader fits into your overall team. I've found that if you want a team that sparks and rolls, you want people who work well together.

Think of a sports team you've seen in which everything fits together perfectly. It may be a hockey team that moves down the ice as players pass the puck back and forth without even looking. Each player just *knows* where the others will be.

They're competent—highly skilled, in fact. And they're committed. And they've obviously been consistent at practices. And a team can skate along on those three things and do a great job.

But when a team has *chemistry*, they're able to do amazing things.

As you bring your leaders on board and move them along, look for ways to help your team develop chemistry. That's when serving in ministry gets to be really fun.

As you recruit leaders, keep these four characteristics in mind: competency, commitment, consistency, and chemistry. When you find people who have all those, they're going to thrive and find joy in serving in children's ministry.

How to Retain Leaders

Recruiting great leaders is one thing. Hanging onto them is another. Here are some tips for keeping your team together for the long haul.

LET LEADERS SERVE WHERE THEY WANT TO SERVE.

If you ask me to work in the church nursery with babies, I'll do it. But I'll do it under protest, and as soon as I can bail, I'm gone.

But if you let me work with fourth- or fifth-graders, I'm your guy. I'll do it forever because that's where I *want* to serve.

My point: If you shove leaders into openings in your program, you'll soon find you've pounded some square pegs into round holes. You won't hang onto those leaders because they're serving in the wrong spot. They don't feel comfortable or capable, and they won't be having any fun.

PROVIDE CAPABLE LEADERSHIP.

In the movie *Remember the Titans*, a football team's captain confronts a talented player about his lack of teamwork. The player tells the captain that he'll be taking care of himself and no one else. When the captain scolds him for his attitude, the player responds with a powerful quote: "Attitude reflects leadership, Captain."

What a great quote! And he's right. Our life and leadership affect our ministry team's attitudes. While you're evaluating potential leaders, they're also evaluating you. How do you treat your team? What are your goals? What's your attitude like? Are you someone worth following?

The life you live will help or hinder your efforts to recruit and retain leaders.

Which life are you living?

1. A Hurried Life—You always feel behind, sacrificing time with family and friends to overcome the feelings of guilt you experience when you're not working. You get headaches, backaches, and stomachaches, and you find it difficult to relax.

The hurried lifestyle can be fatal; the Japanese call it *karoshi*: death from overwork. A hurried lifestyle eventually leads to neglect and oversight of people and ministry details. If you're in constant overdrive, it can be fatal to your ministry.

2. A Heavy Life—You feel as if you're being crushed by a burden of responsibility. You seldom say the word *no*, and you're constantly juggling life's demands. Although your ministry may shine, inside you're like an anchor slowly making its way to the bottom of the sea. Your team wonders if you're ready to abandon ship.

3. A Heated Life—This is the "I'm ready to snap" lifestyle. For these people, little things tend to become big things and overreaction gives way to irrationalism. A lack of patience and loss of temper tell your team that you're unapproachable, undermining your stability as a leader.

4. A Hollow Life—If you're honest about your ministry, you'll admit that there's no purpose, goals, or focus. You're treading water and barely staying afloat, just doing a job rather than serving joyfully in ministry. Be cautious: Your attitude may set leaders adrift to also just go through the motions.

5. A Healthy Life—A healthy lifestyle reflects the things of God, not the circumstances around you. By keeping your focus on Christ as you deal with people and situations you will model a Christlike attitude for leaders.

Discouraged? Don't be. Your leaders already know you're not

perfect (did you think you had them fooled?)—and God knows too.

Pause a moment and consider: Do you find yourself described above? How does your life and leadership impact your team? Meditate on the passages on page 33 as you answer that question.

You can learn a thousand leadership tips and techniques that help you with the business of leadership, but they won't mean anything unless you've dealt with the heart issues of leadership.

What sort of life are you leading? Is it attractive to recruits, or not?

MEET LEADERS' NEEDS.

Yes, you're the children's pastor. But you're *also* the pastor to adults who serve in your ministry to children.

If one of your teachers has a family emergency, whom is she going to call first? Probably you because you've established a relationship with her. You've invested yourself in her and the other leaders who serve with you.

To create a community that offers support to your leaders, do the following:

Think of your leaders. If you're shopping and see something that reminds you of a leader, buy it. Then give it with a special note, such as "I saw this hummingbird poster at the mall and thought of you and your collection!"

Of course, this can only happen if you actually know something about your leaders' likes and dislikes. All the more reason to get to know them personally.

Spend time with your leaders. You're busy. They're busy. But you can never be *too* busy to spend time with people on your team. If you can't spend time with everyone, prayerfully choose which key leaders to pour yourself into, and have them spend time with others.

And remember: "As you go" time is just as valuable as making an appointment for lunch. "As you go" time is the time you spend running to the store and picking up supplies, decorating your fellowship hall, or planning a lesson. So take someone along, even on the short trips. The only way to make this time valuable, though, is to be less concerned about the task and more concerned about the person sitting next to you.

OFFER HONEST ENCOURAGEMENT.

All encouragement is not created equal. It comes down to motive. If your motive in encouraging leaders is to get them to stay in children's ministry, that's wrong. That addresses your need for filling positions but ignores your leaders' needs.

Hebrews 10:24-25 says, "And let us consider how we may spur one another on toward love and good deeds. Let us not give up meeting together, as some are in the habit of doing, but let us encourage one another—and all the more as you see the Day approaching."

That's honest encouragement. It's focusing on others, not manipulating them for our ends.

Honest encouragement lets you put others first. It requires you to focus on your team members so that you can encourage them for specific reasons. "You're doing a great job" isn't nearly as powerful as "I saw how you handled that discipline issue this morning. Great job being sensitive and firm at the same time!"

Realize that what's encouraging for one person may not even register with someone else. In fact, "one size fits all" encouragement may actually backfire with some of your leaders.

Here's what I've discovered: The longer my leaders are on board in our ministry, the less they're motivated by a banana with a note taped to it that says, "You give children's ministry appeal!"

Do my leaders want encouragement? Absolutely, but little gifts and gizmos simply aren't important if that's all they get. What matters more is that they're making a kingdom difference in the lives of kids.

Please understand, I'm not down on giving leaders thoughtful gifts and gadgets. We give them and use those occasions to be

Empowering Moments.

An Empowering Moment is when an encouraging gift connects to a leader's hands, heart, and head. For instance, I once handed each of my leaders a drumstick to hold, and then I showed them a scene from the movie *Mr. Holland's Opus*. It was the scene where Richard Dreyfuss' character had a student use a drum to teach the student how to hear a new beat. The movie connected with my leaders' hearts.

After the movie clip, I pointed out that kids often march to the beat of a worldly drummer all week long. Our job is to teach kids to hear and march to a *new* beat—one that honors God.

At that point a simple drumstick became a powerful reminder of why we do what we do in children's ministry. It became a symbol of an Empowering Moment.

Consider finding out how your leaders *want* to be encouraged and recognized by asking them during the interview process. There's nothing wrong with saying, "Hey, I expect you'll do some great things in ministry. When that happens, how would you rather be acknowledged: with a pat on the back, a mention in the newsletter, or a gift certificate to the local Christian bookstore?" Even if the leader isn't sure, she'll probably at least eliminate one possibility for you.

We use a sheet I put together called "What Floats Your Boat." All of our children's ministry leaders fill it out, and it helps us better meet the needs of all our leaders.

The fact is that we typically encourage others the same way *we* like to be encouraged. But to be effective we have to move beyond that and become people watchers. We need to learn how to encourage others in ways that matter to *them*.

PROVIDE TRAINING.

What does each leader need to move to the next level? Mentoring? Help with specific skills and coaching? A book or conference? Your leaders *want* to serve with excellence; invest in them so they have the opportunity to do so.

You may find that you have a snack-server who's happy to stay a snack-server forever. Great—God needs snack-servers. But make sure you provide opportunities for your snack-server to grow in his abilities even in that role.

One inexpensive way to help leaders grow is to evaluate them regularly. They *want* to know how they're doing. When we value what leaders are doing enough to give them feedback, it says they're doing something important. You won't scare away a valued volunteer if you take time to sit down with her to tell her where she shines and where and how she can get even better.

COMMUNICATE, COMMUNICATE, COMMUNICATE.

I recently learned a lesson about nonverbal communication. A few weeks ago, I was listening to one of our church leaders with my arms crossed and my eyes surfing the background behind him. He waved a hand in front of my face and inquired, "Hellooo...are you OK?"

Ouch, I got nailed.

I'd said I'd listen to his concerns, but only my ears were engaged. My body wasn't, and my body language was telling him that I didn't care about what he was saying. I was devaluing him.

When you connect with your leaders, do they feel cared for or just processed? If you're really bold, ask four or five leaders you trust to tell you the truth. Get that feedback—because if you have leaders who aren't being communicated with in a meaningful way, you can expect them to slowly drift off.

Here are some tips for communicating with your leaders.

• **Communicate with enthusiasm.** A blank expression and monotone voice don't do much to communicate that the ministry you lead is an exciting place to spend time. Radiate joy. Smile. Make eye contact, shake hands, and put a reassuring hand on a shoulder as you pass a volunteer. Be encouraging.

Wait a minute, I hear what you're saying: You're not a touchy-feely kind of person. I feel your pain; that was me five years ago. If you were to invade my personal space with a hug, it would've been like hugging a mannequin: no response, just enduring until it was through. Honestly, I felt like an idiot. Now it just comes naturally. Not the part about being an idiot, but the part about hugging. Reach out and touch a volunteer with a hug, high five, or touch on the shoulder—especially when you're encouraging that person.

• **Communicate with frequency.** I'm a big believer in connecting with leaders as I walk down the hall on Sunday morning. A smile, a pat on the back, a thumbs up as I pass a classroom—as small as those signals are, they count. And they matter.

• **Communicate important content.** Make sure your leaders understand the direction your children's ministry is heading, especially if there's a change coming. If you add a service, switch church leaders in a key role, or move to a new facility, there's always opportunity for misinformation to get around. Communicate what's happening, why it's happening, and how it helps the kids you serve.

RELEASE LEADERS INTO MINISTRY.

Leaders need to have ownership in their ministries and be empowered to make decisions and seize opportunities. Do you trust them to do what you've asked them to do? Have you equipped them to handle it, even if they don't handle it quite like you would?

There's a principle found in Ephesians 4:11-12 that we either follow or we'll flounder. It's the principle of reproduction. We're to be *reproducing* ourselves in ministry.

You see, if we're doing our jobs as children's pastors right, we're working ourselves out of a job. We're finding and equipping people to do the work, not doing all the work ourselves. And we may find that God puts people in our ministries who are actually *better* at doing some things than we are. Great! Set them free to go do great things!

I never tell anyone that something just can't be done, even if I've tried it and found it impossible. God may have waited centuries for someone just ignorant enough of the impossible to do that very thing.

And if they fail, so what? They'll learn from their mistakes, just like we did.

Working with leaders can be one of the very best parts of your ministry. God will draw to your ministry people who love him and who love kids. People who have gifts and skills they want to use and sharpen. People willing to work alongside you.

Will your leaders be perfect? No. But God's power is made perfect in our weakness, so think of it as building in opportunities for God to show up in power.

For more insights into becoming a leader the children's ministry team in your ministry will want to follow, read Craig Jutila's book, Leadership Essentials for Children's Ministry, *Group Publishing, Inc.*

Encouragement Ideas to Try

*h*ere's how some children's pastors across the country encourage their leaders. These are great ways to get started.

1. Hospitality cart—Each weekend, Debi Nixon, the director of children's ministries at the United Methodist Church of the Resurrection in Leawood, Kansas, serves her leaders coffee and refreshments. A special hospitality team pushes a cart from room to room to serve the teachers in each service.   →

2. P.E.T. PROGRAM—The Prayer and Pampering Especially for Teachers program is the brainchild of Becky Johnson, the children's Sunday school coordinator at the United Methodist Church of the Resurrection in Leawood, Kansas.

"We ask parents to take one of our leaders for a year," says Pam Weatherford, the church's special events coordinator. "We give the parents a profile of the leader with his or her birthday and hobbies. Parents send anonymous notes and gifts throughout the year." The gifts are delivered on the hospitality cart mentioned above.

3. PERSONAL TOUCH—Diane Horn, the director of children's ministries at First Presbyterian Church in Santa Rosa, California, sends handwritten notes to each teacher. Diane writes specifically about what she appreciates about the teachers and their ministry. Beyond that, Diane says it's critical to spend time with each teacher to get to know people and to find out how she can pray for them.

4. GOOD GOSSIP—"I talk about my leaders' successes in front of others," says Mark Smith, the children's pastor at Stillmeadows Church of the Nazarene in York, Pennsylvania.

5. PUBLIC PRAISE—Invite your team members to the front of your church for total church recognition.

6. TRAINING—Pay for your leaders to attend local workshops or seminars on children's ministry. Or pay for a volunteer to attend a class, such as a Microsoft PowerPoint presentation, at a community college. The volunteer benefits, and so does your ministry.

7. REPORTS—Ask your team members to tell your church about their ministry experiences. Videotape their stories to share with others.

8. FUN TIMES—Pay for a baby sitter for teachers who have kids. Then take your entire team to a movie.

9. SPOUSAL APPROVAL—Call a volunteer's spouse or send a note →

of thanks for letting his or her "other half" serve in children's ministry.

10. Sunday brunch—Tim Poferl at Northgate Alliance Church in Ottumwa, Iowa, serves a training and encouragement brunch seven times a year on Sunday morning. When Poferl's brunch replaces Sunday school (with substitutes in the classrooms), he has 95 percent attendance. The timing of the brunch encourages an already-busy volunteer force that finds it difficult to come to a weeknight meeting.

11. E-mail me!—Send personal e-mails to your leaders' homes or offices. Rodney Hull, the children's minister at Valley View Christian Church in Dallas, Texas, says, "It's immediate, and it lets people know you were thinking about them."

12. Special parking—Each month, have special designated parking spots right next to the church with the names of your "leaders of the month" posted.

13. Retreat—Chris Smyth, the children's minister's program assistant at Clovernook Christian Church in Cincinnati, Ohio, takes a few of her leaders away on a one-night leader retreat every year.

Remember that encouragement is in the eye of the beholder: Be sure your leaders will like this sort of encouragement before you do it. Ask a few leaders to make sure what you want to do is appropriate and meaningful.

God's Promises for Your Life

FOR THE HURRIED LIFE...

"Be still, and know that I am God; I will be exalted
among the nations, I will be exalted in the earth"
(Psalm 46:10).

FOR THE HEAVY LIFE...

"Come to me, all you who are weary and burdened,
and I will give you rest"
(Matthew 11:28).

FOR THE HEATED LIFE...

"Do not be anxious about anything, but in everything, by prayer
and petition, with thanksgiving, present your requests to God.
And the peace of God, which transcends all understanding,
will guard your hearts and your minds in Christ Jesus"
(Philippians 4:6-7).

FOR THE HOLLOW LIFE...

" 'For I know the plans I have for you,' declares the Lord,
'plans to prosper you and not to harm you,
plans to give you hope and a future' "
(Jeremiah 29:11).

FOR THE HEALTHY LIFE...

"For the kingdom of God is not a matter of eating and drinking,
but of righteousness, peace, and joy in the Holy Spirit,
because anyone who serves Christ in this way is
pleasing to God and approved by men"
(Romans 14:17-18).

three

Safety and Liability in Children's Ministry

by Bill Stout

Ministering to children is an awesome responsibility. In your ministry, you are entrusted with *both* the spiritual *and* physical well being of God's precious and vulnerable children. That means you have to think about subjects that most people would rather avoid: children being hurt by accident or abuse while in your church's care.

As much as we wish we didn't have to consider something so painful, we can't pretend if we're going to have healthy ministries. Accidents and abuse do happen, and our best efforts to share the gospel can be completely derailed by a serious incident. Besides, we want our children to be as safe as possible. We owe it to our kids to be vigilant and prepared for crises.

This short chapter can't possibly cover all the risks and precautions that your church or ministry should consider, but it will help you think through this critical part of children's ministry. Resources for learning more about child safety are suggested at the end of this chapter. You'll also find good ideas for nursery safety and security in Chapter 12: Nursery Notes (p. 136).

Think Proactively

Proactive thinking is your best child safety tool. A safety-conscious attitude should be like background music that's always playing in the back of your mind. Every time you plan or conduct a ministry activity, ask yourself these three questions:

- What could go wrong?
- Are we taking reasonable steps to prevent or minimize risks?
- If a problem occurs, how will we respond?

Share these three questions with your workers during training.

Talk about crisis scenarios, and challenge your workers to think through and respond to difficult situations. As you train workers, distribute and explain specific safety do's and don'ts that apply to the worker's position. Provide concrete procedures about how a worker should respond to problems. Generally, I recommend that any list of procedures open with a requirement to consult a ministry leader as soon as possible.

The Risk Management Process

Use these six steps to avoid letting most problems happen in the first place:

1. Evaluate and prioritize your greatest risks. Tackle the most serious problems first.

2. Gather information to help create your safety procedures from organizations noted on the resource list at the end of this chapter, other churches, your insurance company, and area schools. Also, create response procedures for each of the four types of problems described later in this chapter. Involve a variety of ministry workers in designing your procedures.

3. Ask your senior pastor and leadership team to ratify your procedures.

4. Carefully explain your new procedures to workers and parents before putting them into practice.

5. Once a year review how the procedures are working and what needs to be changed. Ask your leadership to ratify any improvements, and communicate the changes to workers and parents.

Understand the Risks

You may feel overwhelmed at times as you grapple with the

variety of risks facing your ministry—I know I do! It's easier when you realize that most of the risks you'll face fall into the following four areas:

1. MISSING CHILDREN

Children can run away, become lost, be abducted, or be picked up by an unauthorized person. Close supervision by an adequate number of adults is the best defense for the first three situations. Asking parents in confidence to warn you if there are any unauthorized people who might try to take custody of children is a good precaution for the last situation. Using a token system—a process in which you give the person turning a child over to your ministry a "receipt" of some sort to redeem when the child is picked up—to release younger children is an excellent safeguard as well.

2. CHILD ABUSE

Children can be abused sexually or physically. Physical abuse in a ministry setting is rare; when it occurs, it usually takes the form of improper discipline. It's also rare for children to be mistreated physically or sexually by other minors who participate in your ministry. The biggest risk you face in this category is sexual abuse by an adult.

Child molesters have found that volunteering to work with children in religious or secular programs is an easy way to gain trust from parents and access to children. Churches by nature are trusting and informal; sexual predators have noted that churches remain easy targets, even as many other institutions have tightened their safety procedures. There is no foolproof way to deter sexual predators. However, many of the procedures discussed in this chapter and the attached resource list are effective at reducing this risk.

One of the best deterrents is simply open discussion about the issue and the awareness that "it can happen here." A serial child abuser who finds high awareness and many safeguards is likely to avoid or leave your ministry in search of easier targets.

A policy asking newcomers to your church to wait six months before volunteering in children's ministry is another proven precaution. This gives you time to get to know the newcomer's qualifications, and it discourages sexual predators who are only coming to your church for quick access to children.

Program design can increase or decrease risk. For example, holding activities on church property with a group of adult leaders is preferable to activities that take place in a home with just two adults present. (Never plan events with less than two adult workers present.) This does not mean that activities can't take place in homes or other places off-site, but it does mean that extra precautions should be taken, such as extra adults or the presence of a ministry leader.

3. ACCIDENTAL INJURY

The two biggest safety challenges in this category are automotive accidents and playground mishaps. Anyone who drives a vehicle on behalf of your ministry should be required to prove basic qualifications such as a driver's license and proof of insurance. In most states a driving record (known as a "motor vehicle report" or "MVR") can be obtained quickly for a fee of less than twenty dollars. Check with your church's insurance company since many will obtain MVRs for you. Remind drivers of the rules periodically: Seat belt usage is mandatory, rules of the road (including speed limits) must be obeyed, and so on. Plan ahead to avoid situations in which drivers must battle unrealistic schedules, fatigue, or bad weather.

Playground safety is largely a question of modern equipment and good maintenance. Playground equipment manufactured since around 1990 is much safer than older or "homemade" equipment because of new design standards adopted by equipment manufacturers in the early 1990s.

New equipment is expensive but a great investment when safety is taken into account. Modern equipment also makes a positive statement to everyone who drives by your church: This is a place that values kids!

4. DANGEROUS SITUATIONS

If you are involved in children's ministry long enough, anything can happen. I once led a group of teenagers on an outing, and we couldn't return to our dormitory because it was surrounded by a SWAT team! We left, took in a movie, and returned after the crisis was over. Tornadoes, bomb scares, frostbite, high water—the list of unexpected hazards is endless.

That's why ministry leaders must be trained and authorized to make bold decisions that will avoid unsafe situations. Imagine you're holding a picnic in the park when thunderheads roll in and lightning appears. Who has the authority and responsibility to cancel the event or move to a safer setting? What's your bad weather contingency plan?

Leaders hate to pull the plug on fun activities. Often we want to avoid making an unpopular decision, so we hope for the best. Or we doubt if we really have the authority to call off an event because of weather or restructure an activity to make it safer.

Be clear with your leaders that the children are depending on ministry leaders for...well...leadership! They can't evaluate or avoid risky situations on their own. It is *always* better to be safe than sorry when you're caring for other people's kids.

Know Thine Enemy

The most serious type of sexual predator is the serial molester. Serial molesters usually abuse children repeatedly and will assail hundreds of children over a lifetime. Most serial molesters are men, although women can sexually abuse children too. Serial molesters often "groom" their victims extensively before attempting to molest them. *Grooming* means cultivating a child over time so that he or she is more vulnerable to abuse or is less likely to report it. The warning signs of grooming behavior were obvious yet unrecognized in almost every case of abuse I have reviewed.

Examples of grooming behavior include:

• introducing forbidden behavior, such as alcohol or pornography, to the child. The molester then tells the victim "don't tell anyone what we did or you will be in big trouble."

• showering a child with excessive trips, gifts, or money so that the child becomes dependent on the molester. Kids from impoverished backgrounds are particularly susceptible.

• excessive attention given to vulnerable kids. This may include playing favorites, inviting children home, or unauthorized one-on-one activities that are cloaked as ministry activities. Vulnerable kids are those who are needy or troubled in some way or who are loosely supervised by parents.

• disguising sexual exploitation as something else, such as a secret initiation to a club or sex and hygiene education.

• earning the trust of overburdened parents under the guise of showing extra concern for a troubled child. The parents' trust provides the abuser with lots of time and influence in the victim's life.

Legal Responsibilities

Often ministry leaders feel that in a lawsuit alleging sexual abuse, the cards are completely stacked against churches. I don't agree. Courts have generally held that no organization can be expected to protect its children from bizarre or completely unforeseen types of harm. In the event of a lawsuit, courts usually ask some variation of this question: Did the organization take reasonable and prudent precautions to protect the child? If the answer is a clear "yes," then your ministry will not be judged at fault for the injury. "Reasonable and prudent" safeguards are often determined by comparison to similar types of organizations that serve children, both secular and faith-based.

Frequently in cases of sexual abuse, workers use their positions of trust to gain access to children. Most often the children are not abused while the worker is involved in official activities, but rather when the abuser can gain one-to-one access to the child in isolated circumstances. In these cases it is very difficult or impossible for ministry leaders to have known about the abusive behavior. However, churches and other organizations *may* be found liable for this type of abuse under the theory that they were negligent in selecting and maintaining the worker in a position of trust. Organizations have also been found negligent if a criminal background check would have turned up a prior record of child abuse, and the checks were not conducted.

Reporting Evidence of Abuse

Ministry workers may have a legal responsibility as "mandated reporters" under state law to report evidence of abuse or neglect. In most states these reporting laws apply to teachers, child-care workers, and others in positions of trust. Find out the particulars of your state law, and learn who is required to report, what constitutes evidence of abuse, and other details of the law.

Even if you determine that your workers are not mandated reporters by law, I believe those of us in ministry need to report evidence of abuse or neglect. This responsibility includes situations in which the abuse occurs in connection with ministry activities *and* when it is believed to be happening completely independently of ministry activities (i.e. at home).

Children are frequently exploited and exposed to danger in our culture. The church must set an example as a refuge where children are nurtured and protected. Every safe and secure child in your care is a testimony to God's abundant love!

Recommended Resources on Child Protection

• *Avoiding a Crash Course: Auto Liability, Insurance and Safety for Nonprofits* and *Child Abuse Prevention Primer for Your Organization*—Two booklets designed for nonprofits that can be adapted for ministry use. Nonprofit Risk Management Center, (202) 785-3891.

• *The Good Shepherd Program*—A complete safety program for churches including model policies, forms, and training outlines on a diskette ready to be customized for your ministry. NEXUS Solutions, 1-888-639-8788.

• *Better Safe Than Sued*—Written by an experienced youth minister, much of this book is also suitable for children's ministry. Group Publishing, 1-800-447-1070.

• *Playground Safety Packet*—Free and practical information. National Program for Playground Safety, 1-800-554-PLAY. Also check out their very helpful Web site at http://www.uni.edu/playground.

Six Key Areas of Child Safety

*t*he author has trained churches across the country to review risks using the "Six P's of Child Safety." Use this quick summary to start your thinking about the risks in your ministry. Consider making copies for your church leadership to review.

1. PERSONNEL

Your volunteers and paid staff must be screened for suitability and trained in child safety. How do you go about obtaining references and doing background checks? How are staff monitored and supervised? What evaluations do you do? How often? How do you know if someone is a capable, caring staff member?

Workers who fail to follow safety procedures must be corrected, retrained, or dismissed if necessary. How well does your staff know your procedures?

A policy asking newcomers to your church to wait six months before volunteering in children's ministry is a proven precaution. This gives you time to get to know the newcomer's qualifications, and this procedure also discourages sexual predators who come to your church looking for quick access to children.

2. PARTICIPANTS AND THEIR PARENTS

Children and their parents should be oriented about safety aspects of your ministry programs. How are you doing that? Do parents know the limits you place on how and when adult volunteers interact with children?

To the extent that providing such training is practical, train older children and their parents about your safety efforts. Some children are more at risk than others and deserve extra precautions (for   →

OK
TO COPY

example, children with disabilities or children from troubled backgrounds).

3. PROGRAMMING

Program design can significantly increase or decrease safety risks in your ministry. For example, holding activities on church property with a group of adult leaders is preferable to having activities happen in a home with just two adults present. (*Never* plan events with less than two adult workers present!) This doesn't mean you have to cancel all off-site meetings and home-based ministry activities, but it *does* mean extra precautions should be taken. Those precautions might include having extra adults on hand or the presence of a ministry leader.

How well have you designed safety into your programs?

4. PLACE

Where you hold ministry activities can have a dramatic impact on risk. Nurseries and preschool rooms should have self-contained restrooms whenever possible. Playgrounds should be well-fenced. Playground equipment should be modern, safely designed, and in good repair. Windows allow parents and supervisors to see what is going on in activity rooms and nurseries.

If you don't have the luxury of designing facilities from scratch, consider inexpensive modifications that will make your site safer and more inviting. And if you can't modify the design of your site, consider ways to change your programs or staffing to minimize the limitations you face.

Walk through where you hold ministry activities. Is the facility safe? Would parents agree? What about the fire chief?   →

5. PRIVACY

How you collect, maintain, and share sensitive information about children, families, and workers is also important. As you gather confidential information about workers who are screened, you must maintain confidentiality. Do you have a locked cabinet where those files are stored? Who has the keys? What are your written policies about disclosing information? You will need a clear policy on getting and giving references about volunteers and paid staff.

Your volunteers must be trained to recognize when it is proper and necessary to violate a child's confidentiality and report dangerous situations. When facing allegations of child abuse, your ministry must protect the privacy of both the alleged offender and victim. Who are experts in your area who can provide advice and suggestions dealing with legal and personnel issues?

6. PROCEDURES

It's too late to create policies and procedures once a crisis has happened. Be proactive in thinking through and writing down procedures you can communicate to paid staff, volunteers, parents, and all church leaders.

Be sure your procedures cover two areas: how to *prevent* problems, and how to *respond* if an emergency or incident occurs.

And take your policies seriously. Once they're in place, procedures must be followed to avoid allegations of negligence because those safety guidelines were bypassed.

four

Fifteen Smart Things to Do During Your First Three Months

PRACTICAL ADVICE FROM SOMEONE WHO'S BEEN THERE

by Jim Wideman

It's your first day on staff as children's pastor at a new church. The senior pastor has introduced you to the staff, donuts from your first day welcome party have been reduced to crumbs in the bottom of an empty box, and you're sitting alone in your office.

Now what?

How you handle the next few months will have a tremendous impact on the remainder of your ministry. Let's make sure you get off on the right foot.

By the way, this advice applies whether you're launching a ministry from scratch or you're the new children's pastor at a church of two thousand.

1. First, do nothing.

Spend several months not changing *anything* that's currently in place. Use the time to find out what's been done in the past. Ask lots of questions. Observe carefully.

You need to understand *exactly* how the pastor, parents, kids, and current volunteers define a "great" children's ministry. It's likely that their definitions won't be in complete agreement, but everyone will assume *your* definition of "great" matches his or her own.

Focus on discovering what the senior pastor wants in the children's ministry and how that vision has, or hasn't, been implemented.

2. Now fix something—but something small.

Find one small problem and fix it. Don't tackle anything big yet; nobody knows you well enough to trust you, and you may create a bigger problem than you solve.

Are your teachers showing up balancing cups of coffee along with their curriculum? Get a pot of coffee going for them before they arrive, and toss in some donuts, too. Is taking attendance a hassle for teachers? What if one person went room to room counting noses instead of asking teachers to do it? Find something—*anything*—that makes life a little better for your kids, teachers, or kids' families.

You want people to realize that you're actually good for the organization and worth listening to.

3. Connect with your pastor.

When you go into a church to serve as children's pastor, decide you'll be committed to and support your senior pastor.

I believe every church staff member should give the senior pastor what that leader wants. We need to all be working toward the same goal.

I don't see the terms "Children's Pastor," "Youth Pastor," or "Singles' Pastor" in the Bible. We *all* come under the office of the pastor, so we need to share the pastor's vision for the church. In some churches, children's pastors are busy fleshing out their own visions and goals rather than helping their pastors fulfill the larger vision of the church. That's a mistake.

When you come into a church, ask yourself, "What can God teach me through this pastor?" Your teachable attitude will allow you to do significant ministry and also to grow spiritually.

4. Figure out where you are.

Once you understand the pastor's vision for the children's ministry, see if you have the resources you need to meet it. Is the correct leadership in place? Do you have the right tools—the curriculum, furniture, and rooms?

Get to know people. You'll be leading the ministry through your staff (paid or volunteers), so care about them, talk with them, and earn their confidence and trust. The pastor and church leaders may have spent time with you before bringing you on board, but your volunteers don't know you from a load of coal. You have to let them see your heart for the kids of their church and see your support for the pastor.

You *can* lead by virtue of your position; you're the children's pastor, and what you say goes. But you won't be leading long because soon nobody will follow you. *Positional* leadership is the least effective ministry leadership. You want people following your lead because they've decided you're worth following, not just because you have a title.

Summarize on paper how you view your current ministry situation. Summarize where you think the ministry should go, too, and share what you've written with your senior pastor. This is your pastor's chance to fine-tune your direction before you set out to make changes.

And that brings up a critical point: How *are* you getting along with your pastor? and the other ministry leaders?

5. Join the team.

Go to lunch with other people on your church staff, one at a time. Ask what's important to them. Hear their heartbeat for ministry.

Remember that even if the youth group consistently leaves the room you share in chaos, you and the youth pastor are on the same ministry team. Next year you'll be releasing some of your children into the care of that youth pastor. Esteem that pastor and offer your support.

I've become our youth pastor's number one cheerleader, rather than fighting the youth group. I look for ways to serve the youth group. If we want others to respect us, we need to respect them.

That means respecting *everyone* on your team.

The church secretary may save you from scheduling a children's meeting the same day as a school festival. The administrator knows how to fill out reimbursement forms. And the church custodian can turn the breaker switches back on when the building goes dark halfway through your rally.

What matters to these people? How can your ministry work alongside theirs? How can you together move children toward spiritual maturity?

Don't fall into the "Us versus Them" trap. I'll admit that there have been times when I've come home and said to my wife, "Wouldn't it be great if I just had to fight the devil and not also the people I work with?"

That sort of comment reflected immaturity on my part. Don't go there. Instead, think, speak, and act in ways that communicate "We're all on the same team."

6. Determine where you're going.

Set goals for every area of your children's ministry. What do the kids in the nursery need? the preschoolers? Be specific.

Here's a great exercise to help you develop goals: Ask yourself what you want children to do when they're adults. Make a list. You want them to know Jesus? Write it down. Want them to have a servant's heart? Write it down. Want them to be givers? Put it on the list.

Now *you* become those things, and put people who do those things in front of children. Teach children what God's Word says about those things, and model what living it looks like. Let your ministry be a place where children see what God wants them to become and where they can practice serving, giving, and being faithful.

People follow people with a plan. If you haven't developed a plan in your first three months to get from where you are to where you're going, people aren't going to follow you.

7. Communicate with the right people.

Most children's pastors spend 90 percent of their time working on communicating with kids. That's great, but you need to communicate with other audiences, too.

• PARENTS

Create a newsletter that tells parents what you're teaching and what's on the schedule. Since you can't assume that "take-home" papers make it home, you have to communicate by snail mail, e-mail, or fax.

Over the years I've programmed parents to read newsletters by asking them, when they call the church office with a question, if they have the newsletter. They'll say, "Sure, it's on the refrigerator." I'll then tell them where the information they want appears in the newsletter. It'll take awhile, but you can train parents to look at the newsletter *first*, before picking up the phone to call for information.

• VOLUNTEERS

It's a common problem: We want to talk with our volunteers, but they won't come to meetings.

Well, why should they? Are you offering something that they can't get elsewhere and that will help them be better teachers and leaders?

Volunteers who've served for years don't want to hear how to take attendance for the four hundredth time. That's not valuable information. In fact, if you're trying to speak with ministry leaders and all you have to offer is information, why meet at all?

I put information in writing and send it to leaders for review. I reserve meeting times for skill-based training that can't be covered in a letter.

A tip: During your first few months in any ministry, decide how to make the best use of meeting time. Create mailboxes for key volunteers, and use the mailboxes to distribute written information.

• THE CHURCH STAFF AROUND YOU—INCLUDING THE LEADERSHIP.

You've already connected with your senior pastor and taken everyone out to lunch. Great move, but it's not enough.

You have to *stay* connected. Ask your senior pastor for a periodic, standing meeting at which you can communicate what you're doing and how it fulfills the pastor's vision for your ministry. Also, send weekly reports concerning the numbers and how God is using the ministry: attendance, praise reports, and notations of children who have accepted Christ. If your senior pastor doesn't seem to have a clue what's happening over in the children's ministry wing, it's not the pastor's fault. It's your fault for not keeping communication flowing upward.

8. Update job descriptions.

Everyone needs a job description. I like to give every volunteer his or her job description, plus everyone else's job description. When volunteers know where they fit, everyone does better.

Write your own job description first, and submit it to the senior pastor for tweaking. Then write everyone else's description. When your job description aligns with the pastor's vision, and the other job descriptions align with yours, you're all on the same page.

By the way, I always add this final line to all job descriptions, including mine: "And anything else our pastor wants done." That last line makes clear that we're all expected to serve our senior pastor.

Go through job descriptions every two years, and bring them up to date.

9. Build a team.

We say team building is important. We even believe it. So why don't we do it?

The number one reason we don't let people help us is that we're sure they won't do it as well as we can do it. And we may be right.

But there was a time when we couldn't do it very well, either. If someone hadn't allowed us to sorry all over a group of kids and get better, we *still* wouldn't be doing it well.

If you don't allow others to learn by doing—coaching and encouraging them as they go—there's no way you'll build a team. See yourself as a coach and a mentor whether you have a paid staff of two hundred or a volunteer staff of two.

That's going to require that you learn to delegate right quick, but even delegation won't be enough.

Delegation is good; it's letting someone represent you in accomplishing tasks and duties. You need that.

But even better than delegation is *duplication*: creating an exact copy of an original. When you instill your heart and passion in another children's worker, you've gone beyond just delegation and actually duplicated yourself.

I look at our congregation and I can see my heart and goals lived out in people I don't even know. That's because I've poured myself into a tier of leadership under me that has in turn poured itself into the tier of leadership under it. I'm removed a couple of tiers from some of the children's workers, but I see in them my heart for ministering to kids. It's neat.

Here's a tip that'll save you some heartache, too: When you delegate responsibility, also delegate the authority to do the job.

One of the dumbest things I see is that plaque that says, "The Buck Stops Here" sitting on children's pastors' desks. There are a *lot* of places the buck can stop before it gets to us if we'll delegate authority along with responsibility.

Think about it: If you give the nursery worker who checks in babies the authority to determine who gets in and who doesn't, based on the health guidelines, then you won't have people with sick babies lined up to see you.

10. Be visible in worship.

At Church on the Move we have three weekend services. On a given weekend I teach during the first, roam the halls evaluating and coaching volunteers during the second, and go to church during the third. The next weekend I rotate, so over the course of three weekends, I get to see what's happening in each service. And every volunteer gets to see me involved in worship.

It's important for your own spiritual life that you be in worship. It's also important that your volunteers see you as a worshipper. Your actions set an expectation that every children's ministry volunteer should be growing in his or her faith.

Sit right down front, and be visible as a cheerleader for the church, not just for your own ministry.

11. Use the church calendar.

Make sure your church office has a central, master calendar and *use* it. Staying coordinated with other ministries avoids facility conflicts. It also increases participation in children's ministry because families don't have to choose between conflicting meetings.

We've gotten our master calendar to the place where we don't schedule activities that cost money in the same pay period. Realize that if you're going to have good attendance at an event, you have to pay attention to more factors than just dates on the calendar...but start with the dates.

12. Tend to the budget.

Find out how budgets are done, by whom, when, and what the approval process is. Become an expert in the process *before* you have to produce an annual budget. You can accomplish more with money than without it, so don't be shy about figuring out how to ask for money.

To create a budget, ask yourself what you want to accomplish in the lives of your kids. Then develop on paper a ministry that meets those goals. Price the programs and total them up. That's the budget you'll ask for.

Will you get it all? Maybe not—so then look for ways to back off from the best thing you could be doing, but can't afford, to things that will still meet your goals and won't cost as much.

Be realistic. At home you can't afford everything you want, either, especially all at the same time. The church budget is the same way. If the Youth Department is taking care of something they need, you may have to wait in line awhile.

To be effective, have a realistic expectation about how large a slice of the pie your ministry can receive. You may not get the whole hog, but that doesn't mean you can't have a ham sandwich.

While creating your budget, build in ways to give back. I make sure there's a mission education component to our program so that kids learn to give to missionaries. If we're asking people to give 10 percent of their incomes, I want to be sure 10 percent of our ministry income is being given to missions.

Don't easily accept a situation in which children's ministry is funded by income generated by the ministry. I don't think that's wise. There are churches in which 30 to 40 percent of the congregation are children but the budget is less than 10 percent. If your church wants you to be a fund-raising wizard, you have to ask yourself (and your pastor), "Is raising money really the best way for me to use my time?"

13. Shelve the great program you did in your last church.

You arrive in a ministry with some successes under your belt. Maybe you have a program that worked well elsewhere, so you want to do it again in your new church. That may be a mistake.

The program that went well in your last church may not meet the needs of children in your new church. Always start by identifying needs and then finding a program or curriculum that addresses those needs.

This is also why you should be cautious about launching a program just because your denominational headquarters suggests it. Check with your people and current situation first.

14. Be creative and open to change.

Creative people are open to new ideas. They put things together in innovative ways. They tweak and twist and rearrange stuff. And they don't accept the first solution offered just because it's the easiest.

I go to other churches, to malls, and to amusement parks—anywhere kids and their families hang out—looking for ideas I can bring back. What's attractive about those places? What draws the kids? What's fun about the environment?

I've borrowed babies from my staff members, gone to other churches, and checked them into the nurseries to see how long the process takes. I learn from others.

You want to *really* evaluate how smoothly Sunday morning goes for your families? Call a family in your church with three or four kids, and ask if you can take their children to Sunday school next week. See what you put that family through each Sunday trying to get kids to the right rooms. Looking at your ministry through fresh eyes will help you see things you haven't noticed.

That tiny change you wanted to make in your first few weeks may just be adding some direction signs so that people can find their way from one place to another. A small change, but a huge difference.

15. Do the job only *you* can do.

The first priority for any children's pastor is to work on leadership skills. We have to be problem solvers, encouragers, cheerleaders, coaches.

You simply cannot spend all your time in classrooms with kids. Ask the Lord if you're more valuable to your pastor being a leader of leaders and a problem solver than as a teacher of kids. There are other people who can teach kids, but you may be the only one who can do your role.

This can be a tough truth—we're in children's ministry because we enjoy kids, after all. But now you may be in a new role. Are you willing to do it?

five

Partnering With Parents

DEVELOPING A SUCCESSFUL CONNECTION BETWEEN THE CHURCH AND HOME

by Dr. Mike Sciarra

Here's a quick quiz:

• Do you think you can teach a child more effectively than her parents can?

• Do you plan events where parents drop kids off at church so that you can oversee the children?

• Do you seldom encourage parents to teach their own kids?

• Do you ever resent parents because they aren't taking enough responsibility for their kids' spiritual growth?

• Do you only contact parents when there are recruiting needs or when behavioral issues arise?

• Do you sit with kids in worship services so that their parents can "really" worship?

• Do you ever get calls from parents asking why they didn't know about a scheduled event?

If you answered "yes" to any of the above, you may need to develop a better partnership with parents.

You see, your children's ministry is about more than children. It can also provide the best context in which your church can minister to children's *families*.

But for this to be true, you have to develop a creative connection between your church and children's families. You need a strong partnership with parents.

Even if your ministry has already forged a strong partnership, there's probably room for improvement. This chapter will outline some simple changes you can make that will have a huge impact.

CHANGE #1:
Create a Biblically Solid, "Family-Friendly Church" Orientation.

What's your mindset about families? When a family walks into your church building, what do you see?

Some children's pastors see a group of people who happen to live together but who need to get plugged in to appropriate age-level ministries so that the church can meet their needs.

Other children's pastors see a complex, interdependent entity that has needs of its own. True, the individual family members have needs to meet, but so does the family as a unit.

The predominant mind-set in Christian education concerning families has long been that "to strengthen the whole, you must strengthen the parts." That's why at church we deliver Christian education, and often worship, in age groups.

But families need more from church life than age-graded

programs and the occasional all-church activity. *Parents* need more. Many of our church activities actually draw family members apart from each other. We know something is wrong with this picture, but sorting out a solution seems complicated.

The fact is that most ministries focus almost exclusively on individuals. Parents are an afterthought to many children's pastors. Yes, we sincerely want to make a difference in the lives of our children's families—to help parents become more intentional about teaching their children, for instance. But our response to that desire is to tack on one more program that doesn't include both parents and children.

The reality of our lives is that most of the time we're so busy recruiting new leaders and keeping programs running that there's no time to connect with parents at a significant level.

If we want to truly partner with parents, we need a new way of thinking.

• **We can no longer claim to be the experts.** We can't communicate that we're the pros who've set up shop to pump faith into kids, so parents should just drop off their kids and we'll take it from there.

Parents are meant to have the primary role in teaching and discipling their children. Our job is to support parents in their efforts. If parents refuse to do the job, then the church, by default, takes the primary role. But that's supposed to be the exception, not the norm.

• **We need to empower parents to lead.** We need to re-educate parents about their roles as their children's primary faith-shapers. Many parents lack the confidence and skills to comfortably take a leadership role.

You'll know it's working if your stress level decreases, your joy in ministry increases, and you have people on your team who are excited about the same things you are!

What Does a Family-Friendly Church Look Like?

- Families worship, learn, and serve together.
- The church mission statement is intentional about stating the importance of families.
- There are signs of follow-through. A mission statement that mentions families is fine, but if it's in print but not reflected in programming and lifestyle, so what? Is there a Family Ministry Team? Does the team facilitate and encourage family spiritual growth? How?
- Are lessons for kids prepared with families in mind? Instead of just thinking about how children will relate to the lesson, is thought given to how the child can apply what's learned in the context of family relationships?
- A family-friendly church has a family-friendly staff! Talk with your senior pastor and other staff. If you don't know, find out where they stand on ministry to parents and families.

CHANGE #2:
Set and Support Realistic Parental Partnering Expectations.

While it's true that parents are to be the primary teachers and disciplers of their children, it's equally true that the church plays a part too. But we haven't often been effective in setting that expectation and training parents to take on and excel in their God-given role.

If you want to bring about change, start with yourself. If you have children, let others see you model partnering with your children's Sunday school teachers and other adults who serve your kids at church. Be intentional about sharing what differences partnering is making in your family. Encourage other parents to join you, and let teachers know what tools are helpful.

Use whatever soapbox you can find or create to tell parents that it pleases God to see parents leading a family time with God, praying with their children, and worshipping with their kids inside and outside of church.

Here are practical expectations that you might encourage parents to embrace:

• Pray daily with and for their children.

• Memorize one verse together as a family every week.

• Review Sunday school take-home papers. Do the activities together. Talk through the recommended discussion questions.

• Be "with" their children daily—talking, listening, and applying Bible truths to the lives of the children.

• Read Scripture together. It doesn't have to be much, but it has to be clear that God's Word is an important resource and part of daily life.

Meeting these expectations will require resources. Some of them families can provide, but your guidance will be helpful. Some resources can be purchased, but others may have to be created to fit your unique situation.

Some parent-partnering resources you might recommend or provide include:

• family devotion books that get the entire family engaged in an activity, game, or discussion centered on a Bible truth;

• Bibles that children find easy to read and understand;

• children's crafts that double as family-time teaching tools;

• simple family Bible lessons;

• a copy of your curriculum's scope and sequence so that parents know what Bible personalities and stories children are studying in Sunday school;

• a prayer room at your church where whole families can go to pray together anytime they wish; and

• family outings organized by the church, such as day trips, outreach opportunities, and service projects.

What Keeps Us From Effectively Partnering With Parents?

Our understanding—Some churches (and children's pastors) don't understand what God has asked them to do in partnering with parents. We're not to usurp the influence and power of parents, but we *are* to be involved. Scripture assumes that there's a partnership between the church and the home.

We need to provide solid, biblical teaching that establishes the link.

Study for yourself Deuteronomy 6:4-9 and Psalm 78. Review again what Acts and the epistles say about New Testament standards for church leaders. You'll find that to be a leader in the early church presupposed family discipleship. Does your church value it so highly?

Our attitudes—Sometimes our attitudes get in the way. Pastors may not really want parents' input about programming. Some pastors and parents don't think kids and parents should be together for Christian education. Some parents don't want to be with their kids at church.

We've failed to provide partnerships for so long that it seems normal to live without them.

Be careful to not adopt an "us" and "them" mentality towards parents or staff who don't share your vision. Pray for God to change hearts, and allow God to change yours. Be honest with yourself. Ask, "Why do I want to encourage a family ministry?" and "What are my motives?"

Our lifestyles—Families today are stretched for time. Some parents don't think they have the time necessary to provide a Christian education for their children.

What's needed is a "Deuteronomy 6" approach to discipling: for families to talk about and live the reality of God's presence and truth as they walk, talk, sit, stand, and lie down. We need to help parents discover that following Jesus alongside their children is a daily thing, not a Sunday-at-church thing. Challenge people to reshape their priorities, and be willing to do the same as God leads you.

What Do Realistic Parent-Partnering Expectations Look Like?

- You, as a children's ministry leader, are modeling a church-family partnership with your family.
- Resources are readily available to help parents teach their children.
- The pastor frequently publicly encourages partnerships.
- The church calendar reflects partnership opportunities.
- Leaders in Sunday school, children's church, and other children's ministries are trained to reach out to parents.

Make it your personal mission to engage parents at every level of your ministry with children. It's easier to encourage people you know, and when parents understand that you have the best interests of their families at heart, they'll be more open to hear you.

Let parents know you understand that they're busy. Communicate that you aren't trying to place an unrealistic burden on them, but rather want them and your church to be biblical in your approach to Christian education. Share your vision for how God can use them to shape the faith of their children—for eternity.

CHANGE #3:
Balance Age-Level and Multigenerational Ministry Times.

Think about how Sunday morning goes for families in most

churches. Families drive to church together, but once they arrive they're scattered to their separate classes. They worship in different rooms, the children in one place and the adults in another. They don't even *see* each other again until it's time to leave.

If we expect families to be at the church every time the doors are open, yet we don't let families stay together, when are they supposed to be involved in family discipleship activities?

We may be our own worst enemies!

Here are some ways to establish a healthy balance in your children's ministry and church programming. Doing so lets you partner with parents to meet their needs, the needs of their children, and the needs of their families.

• **Welcome all family members into all ministries in your church.** No parent should feel like a stranger or intruder when visiting his or her child's Sunday school class. No parent should feel guilty for wanting to worship together with his or her children. Parents who want to do things at church with their children aren't weird; they're being biblical! Establish a family-friendly culture.

• **Work hard to make each ministry accessible to multiple ages of participants.** This can't always happen, but don't make it common practice to exclude those who want to be included. When churches offer adult-only worship services excluding children, the message is loud and clear: The church alone is in charge of kids' spiritual growth. Work to create programming that's intergenerational and integrated, not isolated.

And if you invite parents to join in a children's ministry program, make sure there's something significant for those parents to do.

• **See families as *families*, not collections of individuals.** Develop simple, user-friendly welcome materials that include children's ministry information as well as "grown-up" information. Develop a children's greeter team that engages and welcomes children, helping them feel at home at your church.

Some programming lends itself to adaptation for integrating the family and home. How about training of family units in communication or safety issues? small group family Bible studies? intergenerational Sunday school and VBS? The goal isn't just to have kids spend time with their parents. Rather, the goal is to equip and motivate parents to be their kids' teachers, shepherds, and heroes!

What Does a Well-Balanced Program Look Like?

- Families are often together at both church and home.
- Families often engage in Bible study, worship, prayer, and service or mission projects. Family members also just hang out and enjoy each other.
- The church deliberately provides time for families to be together. For instance, if a church has a midweek program, there's occasionally an At-Home Family Night in place of the regularly scheduled program.
- The church occasionally hosts a family-friendly activity or party that families can enjoy together.

Challenges to Creating a Partnership With Parents

• WEEK ONE ATTENDANCE

If attendance statistics are a big deal in your church, consider setting that measurement aside for a while. It's hard to predict how many people will come to a "family event." And if families don't attend because they're home spending time together, the parents shaping the Christian faith of their children, that may be a good thing.

New approaches to ministry take time to catch on. Give yourself time.

• KEEPING LESSONS AGE-APPROPRIATE

Teachers may resist leading a class that includes both children and parents. Pastors may not want to have both age groups listening during a sermon.

But keep in mind that parents are built-in leaders who can help their children connect with material. When leading a multigenerational group, you don't have to sink to the lowest common denominator. Aim for the middle, making sure some of what you say speaks to the youngest children and some things challenge the most mature members of your audience.

Even better: Enlist the help of parents in facilitating learning with their children. Let the learning happen in the context of the families.

• THE FORMAT

When you mix children and adults, you tend to hear the volume go up. Potential for distractions goes up, too, but it's worth it.

If you hear someone long for the "good old days" when children were out of sight and out of mind during the sermon, think about what the Sermon on the Mount or the feeding of the five thousand must have looked like.

We're told that there were five thousand men at the feeding of the five thousand, plus women and children. *Hungry* children. Jesus still managed to communicate spiritual truth in a memorable way that families undoubtedly discussed as they walked back to their villages.

CHANGE #4:
Crank Up the Communication.

Regular communication with parents will help you forge an effective partnership with your children's homes.

And I don't just mean telling parents things. I also mean *asking* parents things.

What are the greatest needs of the families in your church? Training? Help with developing family communication? with prioritizing activities and values? with Bible study?

Do parents want mentoring from older, wiser parents? Are there single-parent families who need help with raising children? who need help doing something as simple, but important, as moving a couch or repairing a gutter?

Families will tell you what they need if you'll ask. And as you communicate with parents, you can also share your heart for families, your appreciation for them, and your love for their kids.

Effective communication with parents may also be a front door for initiating other ministry with families. You'll find as you develop connections with parents that you'll be better able to identify what they need, and you'll have the relationships that allow you to become involved.

What Does Communicating With Parents Look Like?

- A regularly routed, easily understood, interesting church bulletin, newsletter, or other publication
- The presence of an open forum for questions and answers, and round table discussions
- A parents' suggestion box located in the main entry of your church building   →

- Frequent e-mails from your teachers to their kids and the kids' parents
- Your presence at child-centered community events, such as sports events, school fairs, and other places where it's easy to bump into and talk with kids and their parents

Developing a partnership with parents is more than a good idea; it's a good, *God-honoring* idea. Parents are, for better or worse, the primary faith-shapers of their children.

We enhance our ability to do ministry to children when we view them as members of a family and respect parents' influence on their children. We touch the lives of parents. And we do ministry in the way God intends us to do ministry.

Top Ten Things to Do to Develop an Effective Partnership With Parents

1. DO recruit a few interested parents to get on board *before* you roll out any sweeping changes or new ministries affecting parents and children.

2. DO check the church calendar and make sure you are not over-stretching families by expecting them to be too many places too often.

3. DO work with other church staff, leadership, and volunteers in your effort to improve your partnership with parents.

4. DO communicate well and let parents know well in advance of upcoming events.

5. DO what you say you believe. If your mission statement says it, do it or change the statement.

6. DO schedule meetings at times that are convenient for families with children whose ages differ.

7. DO welcome all family members into all ministries in your church.

8. DO work hard at being a church that is friendly and accessible to families.

9. DO try new ways of reaching the family, communicating with the family, and equipping the family for service.

10. DO seek advice from others who have traveled the road before you.

And a BONUS tip:

11. DO pray and seek the Lord regarding what he wants you to do!

six

How to Make Changes in Your Children's Ministry

by Sue Miller

Promiseland is the children's ministry of Willow Creek Community Church. If you visit next week, you'll find it's a place where children from infants through grade five feel welcomed, valued, and cared for; a place to learn who Jesus is and how to follow him; and a place where discovering basic Bible truths helps children make right choices now—and throughout their lives.

But believe me, Promiseland wasn't always so promising.

In 1989 we gave ourselves a report card, and there was a *lot* of room for improvement. The kids we struggled so hard to teach said we were, in a word, "boring." The quality of what was taught depended entirely on who was teaching. There was little intentional relationship building because we hadn't helped parents understand the negative impact of inconsistent attendance at our weekend services.

Our volunteers were overwhelmed, undervalued, and in short supply. Our curriculum seemed outdated. The music was irrelevant to our children's everyday lives.

When we graded ourselves on how effectively we were raising up Christ-followers, we had to give ourselves a C minus. So we went back to the drawing board to completely revamp our mission, vision, and strategy.

Our goal: Make our hour with the kids the best hour in every child's week.

We quickly determined that we wouldn't accomplish that goal by sticking with our existing model of children's ministry. Something was missing. We had to make changes if we were going to better serve our kids and volunteers.

What was missing in our ministry was an overarching mission and strategy for what happened on Sunday mornings.

Was our Sunday morning programming for discipleship or outreach? for seeker kids or church kids? How did the various parts of our programming—Sunday school and children's church, for instance—tie together in the minds of children? We didn't have clear answers to these questions.

In reality, we were trying to do too many things on Sunday morning, and our kids were confused about what we were trying to accomplish. Our volunteers were uncertain, and we weren't growing as well as we might have grown because seeker kids wouldn't come.

You see, if you have two or three different programs on a Sunday morning—one for evangelism, one for discipleship, and one for something else—when should a child invite his or her non-Christian friend? We decided we'd do better to take the ninety minutes we had with kids and pick one key concept to teach during that amount of time. And to be intentional about whom we were trying to reach.

As we've discovered at Willow Creek during the past decade, there's a better way.

The Promiseland Story

In 1989 when I went on staff at Willow Creek Community Church, we had a one hour and fifteen minute "Promiseland" for children each Sunday morning.

God was blessing the program. We had one thousand children participating. At first glance, it appeared to be a tremendous success.

But there were challenges, too.

Our weekend service was designed to be relevant, practical, and contemporary to reach adults, especially adults who had never set foot in church before. But while the adult programming was cutting edge, in the children's ministry we were retreating back to adapting existing curriculum, trying to put a new spin on it.

The result: bored kids, stagnant growth, and some unhappy volunteers. The pain was high enough and the compelling need obvious enough that we decided to consider making changes in what we were doing.

I'd like to walk you through the process we found helpful, because it may serve you, too. But first, let me put to rest something I often hear from smaller churches: "Sure it'll work at a huge church like Willow Creek. But it'll never work here!"

When you're in a small church, it's tempting to look at big churches and think, "It would be *great* to have all those resources and be impacting all those kids' lives. And to have all those people to choose from!" You forget that the biggest task of a large church is to try to make things feel *small.*

We work hard to make our ministry feel small and for each child and volunteer to know that he or she matters. Who wants to feel like they're just numbers?

If you're in a small church, of course you want to grow and reach more kids for Christ. But as you grow, don't lose your ability to surround each child and volunteer with people who know that person's name and who will encourage that person. Don't give up the benefits of being small.

But whether you're big or small, you must be *relevant* to your kids' world, and that's where we were running into problems at Promiseland. Our children's ministry wasn't connecting with kids in their real lives, and the consequences were starting to show.

The man who brought me on board, Don Cousins, had conducted focus groups with volunteers and decided to take a hard look at what was working and what wasn't working. Don was realistic. He said, "You know, where we used to be was good. But it's time to turn the corner and redesign our ministry so we can bear even more fruit."

Here's how we moved ahead and made changes in our children's ministry. I'll share the process with you because maybe it's time for you to make changes too.

1. WE DID OUR HOMEWORK.

How do you know if you need to make changes? Step back and take a look at your ministry.

—Analyze the numbers. Is your program growing? Is attendance slipping or stagnant? If you're going to make another leap of growth, you'll need to increase your effectiveness by making a change.

—Are you having volunteers walk out the back door because they feel overworked and unappreciated? Why are they going? What would change their experience?

—Are parents bringing their kids a couple times and then not bringing them back again? If kids don't feel linked into the program, they won't want to return. Is that impacting your numbers? Are you seeing lots of first- and second-time visitors who never get connected personally with anyone? And are you even keeping track of these numbers?

Remember that you can't catalyze change unless something is broken. If people think everything is just fine, they won't believe there's a reason to change. Doing your homework lets you come to your church leadership and volunteers with suggestions for change that fix actual, documented problems.

2. WE ASKED QUESTIONS—AND LISTENED.

For nearly a year, I sat at tables asking key volunteers what life had been like for them since Willow Creek was founded in 1975. It became obvious that Don was right: We were at a critical cross-roads. When your volunteers are saying, "Kids are bored. I think we're becoming more irrelevant in our teaching for our children," you know you have a problem.

Want to know how you're *really* doing? Ask parents and key volunteers who are on the verge of leaving, "What can we do to serve you better?" You'll learn plenty. Sit down with your pastor and church board members and ask, "How can we grow? How can we better serve the families of this church?"

Talk with children, too. Children told us Promiseland was boring, but we wanted to know *why*. The answer children gave us helped reshape our Sunday morning worship program.

"Because you make us sit so long," children said.

So we looked at how long we were expecting kids to sit still, and it *was* a long time. Plus, we were expecting kids to do things they didn't naturally gravitate toward elsewhere in their lives.

So we set out to know our kids' culture. We learned all about their favorite places to eat and have birthday parties, the places where they love to shop, the kid museums where they love to learn. We deliberately borrowed the best from those places so that we could create a place where learning about Jesus Christ and having fun could go hand in hand.

We divided Promiseland between activities, movement, small

groups, and a large group time, carefully running our mission and values all the way through that window of time. The result? Boring no more!

3. WE ESTABLISHED A CLEAR MISSION AND A STRATEGY.

Knowing what *wasn't* working in our children's ministry helped us plot a new mission statement and a new strategy.

We asked ourselves the same questions you need to answer for your ministry: What are you trying to accomplish? What values are you attempting to uphold? Who is your program for? How will you get where you want to go?

The need for a vision statement and a mission strategy is absolutely essential. (See Chapter 1, Setting a Vision, Staying the Course [p. 8] for more specifics.) Take it from me: It's worth the time to decide what you're really about on a Sunday morning and in your ministry to children.

It's how your volunteers know what they're supposed to do and where they're best suited to serve. It's how you make decisions about what curriculum to use. It's how children and their families know which programs to invite seekers to attend.

You may still have a midweek program on Wednesday night, a VBS in the summer, and children's church on Sunday. But a clear mission and strategy lets you be intentional about each piece of that programming—why it's there, what it's to accomplish, and how it fits with the other parts of your program.

Involve church leadership as you establish a mission so that it nests within the larger mission of your church. That way, you'll all walk down the same road, going to the same place.

4. WE EMPHASIZED THE POSITIVE.

As we slowly began changing our ministry, we reminded our volunteers of all the things they were already doing right. This is an important step!

What are your volunteers doing that's positive and effective? Meet with those volunteers as soon as possible to say, "I saw you this morning, and I am so proud of how you served our children and how God is using you in our ministry each week. Here are all the things I saw you doing right." Then list the things you observed. Honor your volunteers.

It's important that you build relationships with volunteers first and then ask what they think is working well. Ask parents what they've appreciated in your ministry to their kids, and pass along those compliments to your volunteers.

If you discover that all parents are happy, all kids are growing, and every volunteer is thrilled, say to yourself, "Wow! This is fabulous! Am I ever blessed that God gave me *this* job!"

But if you discover the need to tweak, or completely remodel, your program, move ahead gradually.

5. WE MADE CHANGES *GRADUALLY*, COMMUNICATING ALL THE WAY.

When we sat down to change Promiseland, we didn't try to fix everything all at once.

We were stuck between the old and the new. Some people wanted to move ahead, but a bunch of people had never seen creative children's programming and didn't *want* to see how it might look. Change was threatening.

We began by making changes in one age group, being careful to use words like *pilot*. I'd say things like, "We're going to pilot this change. We'll check it out and see if it gets us closer to a ministry our kids will love." The word *pilot* was a lot less scary than the word *change*.

When leaders in one part of your program see how successful changes are in another area, they're likelier to get behind the change themselves. Plus, you'll be able to benefit from what you've already learned when you tackle the other age groups.

At Willow Creek we started making changes where they impacted older elementary children, working our way down the line until everyone was on board. The change was gradual and, therefore, both doable by our leadership and accepted by our staff.

Communication is key, throughout the process.

Life goes more smoothly when I come to volunteers and say, "We need to make a change in our facilities, and it's going to require some extra work from all of us. But here's why we're going to do it. Let me help you understand what Bill (Hybels) is thinking, what the Board members are thinking, and why I think it's going to be worth the hours it will take to do it."

When I communicate that clearly with my volunteers about change, I rarely get any push back from them. They understand and sign on, saying, "Yes, that makes sense. What else could we possibly do?"

If you want to make changes to your children's ministry, make sure every volunteer knows *why* and that it fixes a problem or turns a corner to allow for a more effective ministry.

6. WE MADE MISTAKES AND STARTED OVER.

When you're changing programming, you'll stumble a few times. Maybe it's not quite understanding how to use your curriculum or not having everyone quite trained. Or maybe it's that something looks great on paper but doesn't work in your setting.

We once decided to use a puppet to tell the story of Jesus calming the waves. On paper it was great. But when we saw a little puppet turn and face the kids and say, "Peace, be still!" it simply didn't work. The puppet was too small to adequately portray the power of Christ.

We saw the problem during our Saturday night service, so immediately after the service we changed the activity. By Sunday morning the activity was fixed.

As you bring your Sunday school and children's church into a unified, purposeful program, you can expect to make a few mistakes, too.

Don't worry about it. God's grace is sufficient to turn even your near misses into life-changing ministry in your children's lives. And your parents and volunteers will be remarkably forgiving if they understand how you're working to help children discover the love of God.

The mistakes you make are simply steppingstones to crafting an experience for kids that makes it the best hour of their week.

It's All Worth It!

Your children form their first impressions of God and the local church through your ministry, so you want their experience to accurately reflect how awesome it is to have a relationship with the God of the universe. You want your children to grow in their love for God's Word, to grow in their desire to be part of a community of faith, to be committed to using their spiritual gifts within the body.

And if you want all that for your children as they grow older, *now* is the time to share the vision with them. We need to let children see those values in our lives today if we want those values to be part of their lives in the future.

Serving in children's ministry is an honor, a blessing, and a challenge. You have the opportunity to share doctrine and Bible truths with children in ways that help kids listen and learn. You have the opportunity to live out your faith in front of children. And you have the opportunity to make each hour you spend with kids the *best* hour of their week.

It just doesn't get any better than that.

*l*ike all good ministries, Promiseland is a work in progress! But there are six foundational values we embrace and we believe make for dynamic children's ministry. You can discover more about our Promiseland values by attending conferences we host at Willow Creek Church. Call 1-800-570-9812 for details.

1. We're a child-targeted ministry.

Our goal isn't to please our adult volunteers; it's to connect with children. We want to know our kids' culture and plan activities that are age-appropriate and engaging. We look at *everything*—classroom decor, lessons, and music—through a child's eyes so that we create a ministry that reaches, teaches, and loves children.

2. Our lessons will be relevant to kids' lives now.

We want children to discover the relevancy of the Bible and how God's Word speaks to their world and life today. In every lesson we challenge kids to answer two questions that drive home the relevance of Bible truth: "So what?" and "Now what?"

3. We teach the Bible creatively.

We want children to be so fascinated with Bible stories that they're eager to learn more. We present timeless, eternal truth in ways that engage children: video clips, creative storytelling, drama sketches, and other teaching methods. We use variety to keep from being predictable (and boring!).

4. We shepherd children in small groups.

We build relationships with children because we strongly believe that life change happens best within the context of a small, biblically functioning community that meets regularly.   →

5. We keep children safe—spiritually, emotionally, and physically.

Children aren't put on the spot to "know" the Bible or understand a Christian concept. They're never coerced into making spiritual decisions they're not ready to make. Our leaders are positive, welcoming, and sincere. And we provide excellent safety checks as we screen volunteers, provide age-appropriate equipment, and maintain check-in and check-out procedures.

6. And we value fun!

We want children to come back week after week so that we can continue to nourish and nurture their faith. And children (and volunteers) like to have fun, so we build it in!

part 2

Teaching Techniques

seven
Teaching So Children Learn

by Thom and Joani Schultz

First, a reality check: If your Christian education program were admitted to a hospital, where would doctors place the patient?

On the maternity floor because your program is about to birth more classes and greater spiritual depth? On the cosmetic surgery ward, where a tummy tuck might disguise an obviously sagging program? Or even in the morgue because there's no evidence of life?

Hook your education program up to the monitors: Is your program thriving? Are kids growing closer to God? Can children apply God's Word to their lives? Do your volunteer teachers feel they're connecting with children in a powerful way or just going through the motions?

When Christian education programs fall ill, it's seldom because teachers and leaders just quit trying. We *want* children to learn. We *want* children to connect with God's Word. Most volunteers are faithful about preparing and sharing lessons.

Too often, the problem boils down to two potential illnesses: motivation and methodology.

Motivation: What helps children *want* to learn?

Think for a moment about an activity or hobby you love.

Let's say it's gardening. The odds are you became so knowledgeable and involved in horticulture because you *wanted* to dive in and get your hands dirty. Nobody bribes you to pick up a garden spade and do the weeding. No one has to constantly nudge you with reminders that gardening is good exercise for you. You *want* to produce the neighborhood's tastiest tomatoes or perkiest petunias because you're *internally* motivated.

Your desire to learn more, do more, and sharpen your skills springs from inside you. You're looking for ways to become a better gardener.

In children's ministry, it's common to rely on *external* motivation to prompt kids to do things we think will help them grow spiritually. We hand out stickers, stars, badges, and "bucks" to prompt kids to carry Bibles and memorize passages. Those awards are little more than bribes, but they can be effective. In exchange for candy bars or gold stars, kids *do* show up with Bibles. They *do* memorize words.

But what happens when the rewards disappear, as they one day will?

Unfortunately, most of the desired behaviors disappear too.

To build an environment in which children are truly motivated to learn—in which they're *intrinsically* motivated—the first step is to remove the bribes. That clears away weeds that will choke the intrinsic motivation we want to nurture.

The second step is to provide an environment in which children are *intrinsically* motivated to learn. Remember that our goal in Christian education isn't simply to fill heads with facts. We want to see transformed lives, and that means we have to touch hearts, too.

We aren't successful if we simply grow a bumper crop of kids who know a lot *about* God. We're successful when we help children meet, love, and follow God, and when those children desire to continue growing in their Christian faith. We won't accomplish that goal by lobbing goodies and gizmos at kids to "pay" them for reading Scripture, attending church, or praying.

Rather, we need to embrace a methodology that provides fertile soil for intrinsic motivation to take root and grow.

Methodology: What approach provides authentic, long-term learning?

No matter what curriculum you use or create, including the following four elements will encourage intrinsic motivation to develop and authentic learning to occur. The four elements are easy to remember: They're what give kids "R.E.A.L. Learning."

1. The "R" in R.E.A.L. Learning: RELATIONAL

For children, relationships are incredibly important. A relational learning environment takes advantage of that dynamic and includes time for kids to make friends with each other and the teacher. There's positive learner-to-learner talk. Children in these settings hear not only what their *teachers* have to say, but also what their *peers* have to say. And they have a chance to share their own thoughts.

The teacher is less a "sage on the stage" who has to have all the right answers and more of a "guide on the side" who helps kids find their own answers. It's a different role and far more fun for most volunteer teachers.

The teacher is still in charge and making sure kids explore and learn God's Word. But because kids are learning in the context of a room full of friends instead of as separate individuals in a lecture hall, the learning is deeper, richer, and shared. Kids think out loud and explore their feelings, so teachers can provide individualized guidance and help.

In a relational classroom, everyone participates.

2. The "E" in R.E.A.L. Learning: EXPERIENTIAL

Experiential learning, or active learning, fully involves learners. When children "learn by doing," multiple senses are engaged and learning becomes anything but dry and dusty.

Kids make and share discoveries. They get to move and be involved in the lesson and their learning. Their curiosity prompts them to stay engaged and keep digging.

Teachers love experiential learning because it beats the "boredom" factor. When children are assigned the role of "passive listener," they often find something to do to beat boredom…including misbehaving.

Think again of your special activity or hobby. How passionate would you be about it if you'd only ever watched it being done? if you'd been assigned a chair and told to take notes? It's the *doing* that builds internal, intrinsic motivation and helps kids make connections that last.

3. The "A" in R.E.A.L. Learning: APPLICABLE

The test of your Christian education program isn't how well you transfer facts from teachers to kids. The true test is how well kids' lives are transformed.

Your children are bombarded with facts and figures, besieged with information. Your lesson about Jesus dying on the cross is just one more body of knowledge to consider, no more or less important than the math lessons they sat through this week. And there's a test covering the math, so it *must* be important.

If you want children to care about and remember Bible truths, kids need to understand *why* knowing those truths is important. How does Jesus being crucified apply to Susie and Johnny's lives? If kids don't see a connection, the sad fact is that they just won't care.

But when we connect Bible lessons to a child's real world, we encourage their natural curiosity, propelling them to learn and retain. God never intended his Word to be a collection of facts to be temporarily memorized. His Word is intended as a guide for how we should live, for how we can know him, and for how we can deepen our relationship with him.

What will a child *do* with the Bible truth you're sharing this week? If the answer to that question isn't part of your lesson, don't expect your lesson to stick. Find a way to apply the lesson directly to your learners' lives. That's what builds intrinsic motivation to grow deeper spiritually.

And don't get caught in the "gold star trap." It's tempting to measure just what kids can memorize and recite. That behavior is observable, measurable, and can be rewarded. But if children don't apply what they've learned, how deep and lasting will that learning be?

Not very.

4. The "L" in R.E.A.L. Learning: LEARNER-BASED

You provide an atmosphere for intrinsic motivation when you design your educational experiences around the learners, not the teachers. It's just natural that your kids will show more interest if your program takes into consideration *their* interests, *their* learning styles, and *their* attention spans.

Children love choices, and they quickly come to love teachers and classrooms where they have choices and can be creative.

That means we can't keep doing what we've always done.

Lectures don't provide much choice (except between listening and misbehaving!). Neither do fill-in-the-blank worksheets. And anyone who thinks there's much choice in filling out a crossword puzzle hasn't tried one lately.

But learning centers provide choices. So does offering children a selection of activities that all center on the Bible story. And options for a service project that reinforces the day's Bible point provide choice and engage learners in ways that prompt additional questions and study.

Effective Christian education doesn't ask, "How much is being taught?" Rather, it asks, "How much is being learned?"

Take the Test

Take this chart with you and observe your classrooms—from infants through adults. How R.E.A.L. is learning in your church?

RELATIONAL

❒ The leader encourages relationships between learners.
❒ The leader encourages relationships between the leader and learners.
❒ There's discussion in class between peers.
❒ The leader respects and reinforces sharing of thoughts and feelings.
❒ Learners break into pairs, trios, or small groups for discussion.

EXPERIENTIAL

❒ Learners use hearing to experience the lesson.
❒ Learners use taste to experience the lesson.
❒ Learners use touch to experience the lesson.

❏ Learners use the sense of smell to experience the lesson.

❏ Learners use sight to experience the lesson.

APPLICABLE

❏ Learners brainstorm ways to apply the Bible lesson.

❏ Learners write or draw in journals to introspectively apply the lesson.

❏ Learners plan ways to act on what they've learned.

❏ The leader asks about how previous lessons were acted on.

LEARNER-BASED

❏ The lesson offers choices for learners.

❏ The leader provides activities that engage more than one learning style.

❏ The leader checks in to see if his or her lesson has been understood.

❏ Learners have an opportunity to direct elements of the lesson.

How did your classes do? If you see an area of weakness, consider using a curriculum that values relationships, experiential learning, life-application, and a learner-centered approach to Christian education. Or encourage teachers to build in some of the "R.E.A.L. Learning" tips and techniques on page 91.

Tips and Techniques for Adding R.E.A.L. Learning to Your Classrooms

Encourage your teachers to build these techniques into their lessons:

RELATIONAL

❐ Include a time of sharing in each class.
❐ When asking a brainstorming or review question, children form pairs or trios to discuss their responses together.
❐ Ask open-ended questions. They prompt more discussion.

EXPERIENTIAL

❐ Design at least one activity per class that involves more than one sense. For instance, when teaching about the wise men, passing around frankincense or myrrh includes sight, touch, and smell.
❐ Design at least one activity per class that requires children to handle an object or play a game that reinforces the Bible point.

APPLICABLE

❐ Ask children to form trios and discuss: What will I do to live out [restate Bible point] this week at school or home?
❐ Ask children to sometimes journal their answers to that question.

LEARNER-BASED

❐ The leader asks children what they want to explore in future lessons.
❐ The leader knows children's names and major events in their lives.
❐ Learners have "favorite" times in lessons because the methods used relate to the learners' learning styles.

What If a Volunteer Won't Change?

*h*er name is Edna, and she has been teaching the second-graders since your pastor was in diapers. She has told children to sit on their hands for three decades, and she's not about to change now. Period.

What do you do?

Enter into dialogue. It's unlikely that Edna is stuck in the past *everywhere* in her life. Gently probe about why she has updated her furnace, car, or telephone. It's probably because she desired the benefits of making those changes. Point out that children will benefit from her changing her teaching techniques, too—and so will she.

Assume the best. Assume that Edna wants children to grow in their faith. Invite her to visit some R.E.A.L. learning classrooms and see how those techniques are effective in meeting that goal.

Offer training. Don't expect Edna to be successful with a new approach unless you equip her with the necessary tools. Have an excellent training plan in place.

Make the change temporary. Maybe Edna's way *is* best in your unique situation. Tell Edna that you'll evaluate results after she has tried the new approach for a few months. Follow up and talk with Edna as well as her kids and their parents.

Provide a mentor. Person-to-person training is a great way for Edna to "catch" R.E.A.L. Learning methodology.

And if after all that you're still talking to a brick wall, thank Edna for her many years of faithful service, and give her a great retirement party.

eight

Great Games for Kids

by Terry Vermillion

Games may be the most versatile part of your children's ministry programming.

They can be great crowdbreakers, help kids forge deeper relationships, serve as a perfect escape valve for kids' surplus energy, give kids new experiences that lead to learning, act as a fun transition between other activities...

Or they can be a gigantic waste of time.

Yes, children love playing games, but before you add a game to your program, make sure it's a *purposeful* game. Does it lead to learning? reinforce the Bible point or lesson you want kids to remember? set up another learning activity? If not, why surrender valuable time to something that doesn't add value and may even distract from your teaching?

You already know that games work. Decide to make them work *for* you, not against you, by making sure they're contributing to kids' learning.

How to Create a Game That Reinforces Your Bible Lesson

Some curriculums already provide games that connect to the Bible lesson. If so, use them even if they're new to your kids. A game that makes the point is worth learning!

If you do have to start from scratch, here's how to create a game that will tie to your lesson.

• Begin with the point: What exactly do you want kids to learn? Write the point in one brief statement on a sticky note. Be crystal clear in your mind what you want to accomplish. Let's say it's a lesson that makes the point "God makes us a family."

• Think of a game kids *already know* that involves them working together or "being a family" in another way. Tweaking and adapting existing games saves you time and makes explaining rules a breeze because children are already familiar with the basics. In this case you might have them play Link Tag, a variation of the game Tag.

Here's how you play: Have children form pairs, and have each pair link elbows so that they're both facing the same direction and can move together. Have an unlinked child be "It." At your signal the child who's "It" will attempt to tag another child, who will then "unlink" and let the child who was "It" take his or her place. Then the unlinked child will be "It." After a child becomes "It," that child can't tag anyone for ten seconds, which gives pairs a chance to scatter.

• After playing this game, have kids debrief what they experienced. The discussion is what connects the Bible lesson and game. Be sure questions include feeling questions as well as "what do you think" questions, and include the Bible point. For example, these questions could follow the game described above:

- **How did you feel when you were "It"? When you were in a linked pair?**
- **How was being linked with someone like being in a family?**
- **Why do you think God makes those who follow him a family?**

A tip: Make sure any game you have kids play is age-appropriate. See page 102 for information that will help you know if you're on target.

How to Know if a Game Will Work With Your Kids— *Before* You Play It

A game might look great on paper, but how can you know if it'll fly or flop with your particular group of children?

Here are some guidelines that came from an interview with a former Kenner toy designer whose job was determining whether a toy would send parents flocking to toy stores.

- **Start with what already works.** What games do your kids like already? For all the reasons discussed above, tweaking an existing game may be the way to go.

- **Test the game.** Gather your own kids or neighborhood children for a dry run. You may find that you need to clarify the rules or that there's another way to play the game that's more fun.

- **Keep the game simple. And safe.** Complicated games tend to collapse under the weight of their rules. Be sure the game has a clear goal, such as getting over the line or catching a ball, and a few equally clear rules. And any game that's unsafe is already a candidate for disaster no matter how it's played. Is this game easy to understand and communicate? Is it safe to play?

• **Engage kids' imaginations.** Capturing kids' imaginations is what makes games engaging and fun. It also helps if players can't predict the outcome early in the game. Does your game include an element of strategy? unpredictability? If so, you may have a winner!

Competitive and Noncompetitive Games

Competition isn't bad in and of itself. Life is full of competitions, from grades to landing a starting spot on a sports team or first chair in an orchestra. Competition can sharpen skills and motivate some kids to excellent performance.

The problem with competition is that you create winners and losers. Ask yourself: Does competition teach what you want kids to learn in your children's ministry? Does beating another team communicate grace? Do you want some kids to feel like winners at the expense of children who are therefore losers?

I believe noncompetitive games are better for children because they promote self-confidence and self-esteem. Noncompetitive games are kind. They promote group-building. They involve co-operation. And they allow everyone to participate, not just those who have a special skill. In most cases, noncompetitive games fit better with the church mission.

Terry Orlick, an author who believes in the importance of noncompetitive games, has published two books of cooperative games. The back cover of his book *The Second Cooperative Sports & Games Book* explains his philosophy: "Terry Orlick's approach to sports is simple: When people play together and not against each other, everyone has more fun." [1]

Be warned: Competitive kids will often resist cooperative play. They'll try to add competition to the game, or they'll complain that since no one wins, the game is pointless.

To change this tendency, start by introducing familiar cooperative games. Tag works if you'll keep the play area small so that a child's ability to run and dodge quickly doesn't become a factor.

If you do play competitive games, change the rules so that winning isn't important. For example, play softball in a noncompetitive fashion. When the batter doesn't hit the ball after three tries, the batter becomes the first baseman. The first baseman moves to second base and so on. The right fielder runs in to join the batting lineup.

In addition to playing competitive games that you've altered, try cooperative games like those found in *Everyone's-a-Winner Games for Children's Ministry* (Group Publishing, 1995).

How to Deal With Competition

There may come a time when you have to play competitive games. Maybe your children's ministry group visits another church that has planned an entire program of competitive games. Or you end up coaching a children's basketball team.

If this happens, start by setting a few simple rules:

1. No name-calling. Don't let children put down other children or themselves. This includes times when children make mistakes during the game and call themselves "dummies."

2. No unnecessary roughness. Competition can bring out the bully in some kids—and adults. If you see a cheap shot in a basketball game, call it. If you see relationships being damaged by competition, intervene.

3. Insist on good sportsmanship. Always. And look for actions and attitudes that exemplify good sportsmanship in your opinion, and praise children who demonstrate those. Set clear guidelines.

Before competitive play commences, explain that God loves every child on all teams. Have children find something they like about the other team and tell the other players. Encourage children to cheer a good performance, no matter which team does it. Have children learn and act on this rule: Winning isn't the important thing; loving each other is.

How to Organize a Game Day

Want to do games in a *big* way? Spend an entire morning playing, or organize a special game session. Here are some things to keep in mind:

• Vary the energy level of the games. Start with a moderately energetic game, and then move to a highly energetic game. Do a quiet game next. Then finish with active games.

• Have children begin the game time playing nonthreatening, whole-group games. The least threatening games for children include the whole group, are controlled by one leader, and don't require touching. These games let children move around a lot in a short period of time.

• Then play games for small groups. These games help children recognize faces without requiring kids to get too close to one another. An example of this sort of game is "Musical Instruments," found in *Fun Group Games for Children's Ministry* (Group Publishing, Inc., 1990).

Form teams of two to ten players. Have each group move into its own space (different rooms, if possible) and, without any props or materials, create a musical instrument complete with sound and movement. Give groups exactly five minutes. Then have groups each perform their instrument. Form different groups and play again.

• Finally, play games that involve interaction between pairs of children. At this point you can introduce games with appropriate touching. Even upper-elementary-age children will hold hands at this point. But playing a game that requires fifth-graders to hold hands at the beginning of a game time won't work—most kids will refuse to do it.

Games for Young Children

Children usually don't play with other children until halfway through their third year. Until then, most children play alongside each other, each playing his or her own game. Sometimes you see two-year-olds pass toys back and forth and copy each other's actions, but they're seldom really playing together.

Many two-year-olds will play a one-to-one game, such as Pattycake, with an adult. But most two-year-olds will refuse to play the same game with another two-year-old. For this age group, games for children to play "alone with the group" are best.

For example, play singing games in which each child does hand motions to a song. Or make up games in which you give simple directions to the children and have them mimic your actions. For example, ask:

- **Who can touch a finger to a knee?**
- **Who can stomp their feet?**
- **Who can jump up and down?**
- **Who can sit down?**

Try this game with two- and three-year-olds: Together sing the words "God loves me and God loves you" to the tune of "Twinkle, Twinkle, Little Star," singing the same phrase six times. When you sing the word *God*, point to the ceiling, and encourage the children to also point to the ceiling. When you sing the word *me*, point to yourself. When you sing the word *you*, point to someone else. If the toddlers want to keep playing, substitute the names of children in the group for the words *me* and *you*. For example, sing, "God loves Kelly and God loves Lee," and point to those people as you sing. Make sure you use everyone's name.

This game is a community-builder. How? Most community-builders involve working together as a group to accomplish a purpose. This game works as a community-builder because it gives two-year-olds a common experience. Children see each other and the leader as nonthreatening. (They see that the leader isn't going to grab their hands and make them do something.) They develop a relationship with the leader. And when you use their names in the song, it helps them learn the other children's names while building their self-esteem when they hear their own names sung.

Four- and five-year-olds are more capable of group games. The developmental chart on page 102 explains the developmental and social attributes of this age group.

A game I like to play with preschoolers is called Touching Together. This game encourages preschoolers to share an object and work together to accomplish a goal. It also offers a nonthreatening way for four- and five-year-olds to be close and touch each other.

Before children arrive, assemble five or more objects of increasing size. For example, you might choose a pencil for the first item, a block for the second item, a book for the third item, a large-format magazine for the fourth item, and a carpet square as the last item.

When you're ready to play, lay the pencil on the floor. Then ask: **How many of you can put one finger on the pencil at one time?** Children will giggle as they all try to wiggle together to touch the pencil.

Then ask: **How many of you can put *two* fingers on the pencil? How many can put a nose on the pencil?**

Then remove the pencil and put down the block. Ask: **How many of you can put one finger on the block? one elbow? one knee?**

With the book, ask: **How many of you can put one finger on the book? one heel? one ear?**

Continue with the rest of the objects and suggest larger body parts. Finish by asking: **How many people can stand on the carpet square?**

Endnote

1. Terry Orlick, *The Second Cooperative Sports & Games Book* (New York: Random House, 1982).

Choosing Games for Different Ages

*n*ot sure which games work best with which ages? These types of games work with these age groups:

TWO- AND THREE-YEAR-OLDS

Games can involve jumping, crawling, walking, and hand motions as long as the game doesn't depend on precise movement. Look for games that are simple to explain and can be demonstrated during the game. Games in which everyone performs alone are best. For example, Simon Says works well with this age group.

FOUR- AND FIVE-YEAR-OLDS

Games can include running to and from a point, hopping, jumping forward and backward, or throwing and catching a large ball. Children will work with a partner. "Pretending" games, such as "Can you pretend to be a cat?" are good choices.

SIX- TO EIGHT-YEAR-OLDS

Play games that have a variety of small and large movements. Directions can include five or six activities at one time. At this age, children think games with rhymes and chants are fun.

NINE- TO TWELVE-YEAR-OLDS

Games can be physically active with complicated rules. Play games that have teams or small groups. Look for games that have an obvious ending. For example, Tag doesn't have an obvious ending. Children could play it for hours and never know when to stop, except when they are tired of playing.

Older children can move and use their bodies in a variety of ways such as hopping, running, skipping, and jumping. Upper-elementary-age children can play games that require fine motor control.

nine
Adventurous Art and Creative Crafts

by Mary Gray Swan

The world appears to be divided between two sorts of people: those who just *love* crafts, and those who think "chenille wire" is a 1960s girl group. People in the second category simply can't understand the appeal of craft projects.

So children's ministry leaders who fall in the second group shy away from crafts, and that's a shame.

Crafts are a wonderful way to connect with children and reinforce a Bible lesson or story. Crafts let children express their knowledge, thoughts, and opinions. And whether it's in Sunday school, vacation Bible school, or an after-school program, children need opportunities to explore and increase their creativity.

The Importance of Art and Creativity

Our God is creative and has instilled creativity in us as well. We can use that creativity to praise and honor God, connect with others, and express ourselves. We need to value and encourage creativity!

But how do you encourage your leaders to think creatively and, in turn, to encourage their children to think creatively?

When it comes to art and crafts, it begins with the projects you select. We've all suffered through "arts and crafts" that were no more than following a series of instructions that left everyone's project looking exactly the same. That's not art! And it's not creative!

Creativity recognizes that there's more than one way to do most things. And it makes room for diversity and personal interpretation.

Thinking creatively requires that we ask questions that allow for more than one answer. When you ask children, "How many different colors do you see in the sky today?" they'll actually peer up at the sky and think about the question rather than just mumbling "blue."

We must encourage children to look for the unexpected and develop their ability to describe what they experience. Our classrooms must be places where it's safe to explore options and to experiment with new ideas. When we do this, we're developing the creative side of children.

Enhancing a child's creative ability enhances the child's physical, mental, social, emotional, and spiritual growth. A seemingly uncomplicated activity such as painting at an easel offers children several developmental opportunities. They develop eye-hand coordination as they dip their brushes in paint, make a mark on the paper, and then manipulate the brush to make a design. They develop their small muscles as they control the brush with their fingers. They learn more about color, texture, shape, line, and form. They interact with other children and learn social skills. They express their feelings through their design. And all of this may result in a deeper relationship with God as they express themselves and a children's leader helps the child see what God has painted in nature.

Whew! A lot can happen with a seemingly "worthless" activity such as painting at an easel.

Doing Art With Children

When you do arts and crafts with children, you can't just explain the project and plop the art supplies on a table. Instead, follow these twelve pointers:

1. Allow plenty of time. Don't rush the creative process.

2. Provide alternative activities for children who finish quickly. Some children work more quickly than others do.

3. Provide an appropriate work space. Use bare floors or table tops that have plenty of elbowroom. Cover the work area with newspaper or a plastic tablecloth to protect surfaces and make for easy cleanup.

4. Be prepared. Children won't wait patiently while you gather materials or reread instructions. And always try the craft first to make certain that it works and that you understand it.

5. Start by having children wash their hands. Cover children's clothes with old shirts, smocks, or aprons.

6. Work near water. If a sink isn't handy, have buckets of soapy and clear water on hand with a supply of towels.

7. Have children help with cleaning up. But before you assign specific cleanup tasks, know which children can do which tasks. Don't have very young children clean up the paint. Set children up for success, not failure!

8. Never let children work with electrical appliances. Always carefully supervise any art activities that involve heat.

9. Choose activities that allow children to creatively express themselves. Vary activities by providing paper in various shapes

and sizes. Give interesting backgrounds for children to work on such as cardboard, sandpaper, wood, or fabric.

10. Use repetition. The same art activity can take on new form and meaning as children grow and use different materials. Consider combining two art projects, such as drawing with chalk and finger painting.

11. Affirm children. Make positive comments about the lines they draw, the forms they create, the colors they choose, and the thought they've put into an art project. Compliment the process, not the final results. Don't touch up a child's artwork to "improve" it, and never, ever ask, "What is it?"

12. Let children be creative. Let children decide (within reasonable limits) how to use the art materials. Don't present a right and a wrong way to do an art project. It's true that there's just one correct answer to the question, "Who died on the cross to redeem us?" but there's not one correct way to draw a picture of Jesus.

CREATIVE IDEA!

Colorful Glue

To make using glue more fun, add a couple of drops of food coloring to a bottle of white glue. Prepare multiple bottles of glue, each in a different color.

The Well-Stocked Art Cabinet

You can offer a variety of creative art experiences to children of all ages with these basic supplies:

• Paper of all kinds—construction paper, newsprint, manila folders, poster board or tagboard, shelf paper, and newsprint.

• Writing materials—crayons, washable felt-tip markers (both broad- and fine-point), paint markers, chalk, and pencils.

- Painting materials—tempera paint, watercolors, and paint-brushes.
- Scissors—for right- and left-handed children.
- Adhesives—white glue, tape, and paste.

Add to your art supplies by asking for donations. Some children's pastors periodically send a list of needed supplies to the children's parents. On this list you might want to include newspaper, wallpaper scraps, scrap paper from print shops, fabric scraps, buttons and other sewing trims, wrapping paper, ribbon, scraps of wire, yarn, magazines, catalogs, spools, egg cartons, empty disposable towel rolls, and boxes.

Throughout the year, create crafts with these items. Then at the end of the year, consider disposing of all leftovers you don't want to keep by asking the children to build a tower or create some other structure.

If you have an adequate budget, you might also want to buy aluminum foil, wax paper, clear and colored plastic wrap, lunch bags, paper plates, doilies, drinking straws, and modeling clay. And when you go shopping, buy these items at discount stores or supermarkets where the prices are considerably lower than at school-supply or office-supply stores.

Organizing Your Art Supplies

Nothing derails an art project more than *almost* being able to find the supplies you were *sure* were in the cabinet…somewhere.

Once you have supplies, get organized. Arrange basic supplies on shelves that are accessible to children. Label the shelves so that children can easily return unused materials to their proper places. For example, I put a picture of markers on the shelf (or box or can) where the markers go so that even young children can easily find the space.

Or arrange supplies on shelves where children *can't* get to them. Some churches keep supplies in a teacher-only area where leaders can "check out" supplies to later return.

Use baskets, bins, trays, and clear plastic boxes to organize supplies. Recycled plastic peanut butter jars work well for holding small items such as beads and buttons. Use recycled plastic ketchup and syrup bottles to mix powdered tempera paints. Pie pans and plastic frozen-dinner trays are also ideal for holding miscellaneous art supplies.

Some churches create a supply room for teachers. If you do this, consider recruiting a volunteer to keep the room organized and to order supplies when they run low. Each Sunday, this person can also gather all the materials each teacher needs and put each teacher's materials into a plastic carryall. If you are able to provide such a volunteer, your teachers will love you for it.

An alternative is to store supplies in each Sunday school room. This makes for easy access, but it's difficult to monitor what supplies are in short supply.

Art With a Conscience

Once you start collecting supplies, you'll quickly become a "pack rat." Before you throw away anything, you'll ask yourself if you can use it for an art project. Taken in *moderation* this is not only good stewardship, but your children will learn from your example that they shouldn't mindlessly throw things away.

An area that concerns me is using food in creative art. Many art-and-craft ideas—such as vegetable printing, bean-and-pasta collages, and pudding finger painting—require food that's wasted. In a world of starving people, do we really want children playing with food?

We also send mixed messages to young children when we want them to eat (and not play with) food at the dinner table and then play (but not eat) food during an art activity. We aren't doing parents any favors if we convince children that finger painting with food is great fun. They *will* try it at home!

Try to find alternatives to using food in art projects. For example, instead of vegetable printing, use kitchen utensils, keys, combs, blocks, rollers, or soap. Instead of bean-and-pasta collages, use sequins, beads, and fabrics. And finger painting is as easily done with commercial paint or with a homemade substitute as it is with pudding.

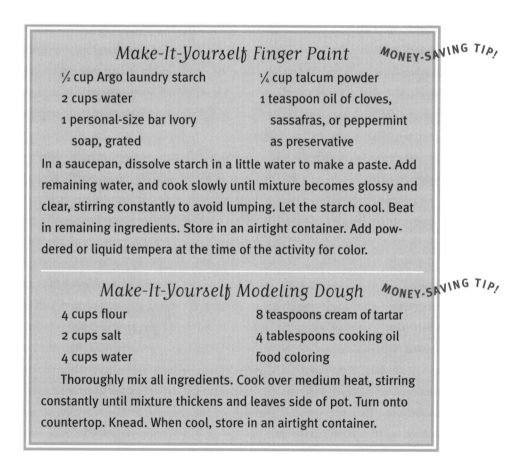

Make-It-Yourself Finger Paint   MONEY-SAVING TIP!

½ cup Argo laundry starch

2 cups water

1 personal-size bar Ivory
  soap, grated

¼ cup talcum powder

1 teaspoon oil of cloves,
  sassafras, or peppermint
  as preservative

In a saucepan, dissolve starch in a little water to make a paste. Add remaining water, and cook slowly until mixture becomes glossy and clear, stirring constantly to avoid lumping. Let the starch cool. Beat in remaining ingredients. Store in an airtight container. Add powdered or liquid tempera at the time of the activity for color.

Make-It-Yourself Modeling Dough   MONEY-SAVING TIP!

4 cups flour

2 cups salt

4 cups water

8 teaspoons cream of tartar

4 tablespoons cooking oil

food coloring

Thoroughly mix all ingredients. Cook over medium heat, stirring constantly until mixture thickens and leaves side of pot. Turn onto countertop. Knead. When cool, store in an airtight container.

Age-Appropriate Arts and Crafts

I've categorized the following art activities by age level. Although the crafts for older children are inappropriate for preschoolers, the opposite isn't true. So-called preschool crafts, led with enthusiasm, have intergenerational appeal.

PRESCHOOLERS

• *Blot art*—Fold art paper in half and reopen. Have each child randomly drip a small amount of tempera paint onto his or her paper, using different colors for more colorful art. Have kids close their papers and gently rub the outside to spread the paint on the inside and then open to reveal a mirrored design.

• *Spatter painting*—Have each child lay an object such as a leaf on a piece of paper. Hold a piece of screen above the paper. Have the child dip a toothbrush or vegetable brush in tempera paint and gently brush over the screen so the paint spatters onto the paper below, then remove the object.

• *Crayon melting*—Place a piece of wax paper (about twelve inches long) on top of a stack of newspaper for each child. Have each child scrape crayon shavings from several colors of old crayons onto his or her wax paper with a nonserrated plastic knife. Have each child fold the wax paper in half with the shavings on the inside and cover the wax paper with a paper towel. Then have an adult iron with a warm iron. The crayon shavings will melt together to look like stained glass. Then have children cut the wax papers into shapes or frame them with construction paper.

• *Bubble painting*—Secure a large piece of newsprint on a fence or between two poles. Add several drops of food coloring to bubble-blowing liquid. Let children blow bubbles in the direction of the paper. Then use the paper as gift wrap for gifts to parents or as the background for a bulletin board.

Crafts for All Ages

You can do creative activities with children of all ages. Descriptions, required materials, procedures, and age adaptations appear below:

ACTIVITY	MATERIALS	PROCEDURE	AGE ADAPTATIONS
Drawing	Use different kinds of paper, crayons, pencils, felt-tip markers, and colored pencils.	Let children do this while sitting on the floor or at a table.	Expect only scribbles from toddlers. Older children may enjoy combining media.
Brush painting	Use 18x24-inch paper, tempera paint, and brushes of assorted widths.	Have children do this at easels or on a table or floor.	Use only one or two colors at a time for young children.
Finger painting	Use a Formica countertop, cookie sheet, or cafeteria tray; finger paint; powdered tempera; and large sheets of butcher paper or newsprint.	Let children paint directly on the countertop, cookie sheet, or tray. When finished, lay a piece of paper over the finger paint to make a picture.	This art activity works well with all ages. Let even two-year-olds finger paint on the surface.
Chalking	Use manila or construction paper, colored and white chalk, and hair spray.	Have children dip chalk in water for a different effect. Have an adult spray the picture with hair spray, which keeps the art from smudging.	Expect only scribbles from young children. Combine chalking with finger painting for older children.
Collage	Use cardboard or paper plates for background material. Provide paper scraps, magazines, fabric scraps, and glue.	Let children arrange items on their background materials as they wish.	Pour glue into butter lids, and let young children dip items in the glue and then place the items on the background paper.
Modeling dough or clay	Use dough or clay. Consider providing sculpting tools.	Let children manipulate as desired.	Modeling dough or clay is difficult for young children.

KINDERGARTEN–THIRD GRADE

• *Leaf pounding*—Arrange green leaves on a piece of wood or Masonite. Place a piece of unbleached muslin, heavyweight interfacing, or a similar light-colored fabric over the leaves. Secure with tape at the edges so the fabric won't move. Gently hammer the fabric with a mallet until the chlorophyll from the leaves comes through onto the fabric.

• *Melted-crayon painting*—This activity requires adequate supervision but is lots of fun. Remove paper from old crayons and sort colors into muffin tins or small metal containers such as cat-food cans or pudding cans. Cover the bottom and sides of an electric frying pan with aluminum foil for protection. Then place crayon cups in the frying pan. Turn on a low setting, and allow the crayons to melt. Give children each a work surface such as cardboard, heavy paper, tree bark, or a piece of scrap wood. Warn children that the cups are hot. Have kids use cotton swabs to paint the melted crayon wax onto the work surface. The crayon will harden when it hits the work surface, but it will leave a texture.

GRADES FOUR–SIX

• *Ping-Pong-ball painting*—Cover a large surface with butcher paper. Dip Ping-Pong balls into liquid tempera paint, and have kids play "Keep the Ball on the Table." Drop the paint-covered balls onto the middle of the paper, and have children blow the balls around. Use the final product for a tablecloth, a bulletin board background, or wrapping paper.

• *Juice-can lid ornaments*—Save lids from frozen fruit juice cans until you have at least one per child. Cut a circle the same size as the lid out of paper for each child. Have children draw designs on their papers. Give each child a juice-can lid, a block of wood, a nail, and a hammer. Lightly attach the paper designs to the lids with rubber cement. Have children gently tap holes through their papers into the lids at even but short intervals (about a quarter inch) until the design is completed. Remove the pattern. Punch a final hole in the top of the lid. Hang with ribbon or yarn.

ten

How to Lead Music With Kids

by Mary Rice Hopkins

There's music in heaven.

We know this is true because when John describes the throne room of God in the book of Revelation, he paints a vivid picture of elders bending before the Lamb, singing a "new song."

Angels echo the praise, as does every creature in heaven, and on earth, and under the earth, and in the sea. Music delights our God (Revelation 5).

And in some way, God has created in us the capacity to experience joy through music too. Especially children, who haven't yet learned to question their musical abilities or worry about hitting just the right note, find that singing is a delightful way to praise God.

That's one reason your children's ministry will be richer if you include a musical component. Another reason is that music makes Scripture passages memorable; add a tune to a verse you want children to learn, and they're likelier to remember it later. Plus, music is fun!

To be effective leading music with children, you and your teachers must have three things ready: yourselves, the music, and your children.

Preparing the Music

What do you want to accomplish with a time of music? To help children memorize a Scripture passage? worship? burn off energy in a fun, expressive way? It's important to select music with your purpose in mind.

When selecting music to accompany a Bible lesson, be intentional about the themes and moods of songs you select. Carefully use music that reinforces the point of your Bible lesson. It's easy to let twenty minutes slip away doing fun motion songs, only to discover there's no time left for the songs that teach.

Introducing the songs by reading and briefly explaining a Scripture passage helps children make the connection between what they're studying and what they're singing. Don't assume the connection will be obvious, even to adults!

And consider varying from the traditional "sing first, study last" approach to teaching. It may be more effective to study first and then sing or to incorporate music and motions several times throughout the class session.

In addition to meeting your purpose, music must also be age-appropriate. When it comes to selecting age-appropriate music, here are some guidelines:

• **Evaluate the lyrics.** For young children, choose songs that include few words and simple or repetitive phrases. Avoid songs that contain abstract thoughts, such as "Jesus is in my heart." Songs that tell stories are usually great for younger children, and kids love to sing songs with which they can move and express themselves through motions.

Older children have a larger vocabulary and a greater ease dealing with abstract concepts.

And while it's great to have fun and include "silly songs" in your song time, you'll want to be intentional in including songs that help make your Bible point or connect to your Bible story. Read the lyrics carefully before teaching a song to children; those lyrics may stay with children for a very long time.

• **Evaluate the musical style.** Younger children prefer easy-to-sing, singsong styles of songs. But don't sell children short—even elementary-age children are listening to the more high-energy, strong percussion music we associate with junior high and high school young people. When selecting music, be sure you include several styles, and don't be afraid to experiment with "older" styles of music to see how your children respond.

Even at a young age, children may have developed a strong preference for specific musical styles. Including a variety of styles helps engage more children.

Preparing Yourself to Lead Music With Children

Some of your adult leaders might not be gifted musically. They may feel awkward leading music yet find that the children in their classrooms want to sing.

Here are some tips to help even nonmusical leaders be better prepared to help lead children in singing:

• **Never apologize for your lack of musical abilities or preparation.** Approach each session with prayer and confidence. Do what you can do, and give the time to God to use as he will.

• **Consider letting selected *children* lead the singing.** This requires preparation, but engaging children as song leaders may provide not only a time of singing or music, but a valuable discipling opportunity as well. And you may have some tremendously musical children to tap!

• **Remind your teachers that when leading children, they needn't be overly concerned about their voice or musical skills.** Adult leaders probably sound fine to the children, and a leader's enthusiasm will more than compensate for any shortfall in musical training or aptitude.

• **Master the lyrics and music.** Leading singing isn't an area in which a teacher can "wing it" and hope for the best. A lack of preparation is not only flustering for a leader, it also shortchanges the children and robs them of a chance to enter wholeheartedly into worship or learning.

• **Rehearse with any CD or tape you intend to use.** The time to practice using the CD or tape player and to cue up music recordings is *before* children arrive.

• **If you're using a split-track CD or tape, set the balance so that children don't hear just you.** Let them also hear the lyrics softly in the background. Some children will be more comfortable joining in singing if they're confident nobody will be able to pick out their voices.

• **If you're leading music alone, draw the children as close as possible to you.** Sit on the floor or in a tight circle. Children love to be close to the action, especially if you're playing an instrument. Here's where having learned the music and lyrics well really pays off, because every move you make will be closely watched. Already knowing the songs communicates that they're both easy and important. And it lets you watch the children and keep them engaged.

• **Pick your location carefully.** When leading a small group of children, don't use a main sanctuary that seats five hundred; your little group of children will feel lost and ill at ease lined up in a single pew. Instead, select a smaller, comfortable room where your voices won't get lost in the void.

• **If you're leading a large group of children, gather the children around you in a "theater in the round" arrangement.** In doing so you'll make sure that no child is more than a few rows away from you and, therefore, children stay more involved. This is also a good time to consider recruiting student helpers to assist you. It's a bonus if your helpers are peer leaders in the larger group because children will often follow the example of their peer leaders and focus more closely. And if you're working with a *particularly* large group, recruit additional adult leaders who know the music well and who understand your objective for the song time.

• **And remember that a large group will usually follow your lead.** If you want them to sing loudly, sing loudly yourself. If you want them to sing quietly, sing quietly yourself.

Preparing Children to Enter Into Times of Music

Whether you're leading a small or large group, and you're an experienced song leader or a first-timer, you're going to encounter children who are reluctant to sing and do motions.

Here are some tips for getting reluctant children involved:

• **Unless they're disrupting others, don't force them to participate.** Children "opt out" of participating for lots of reasons, some of them very personal and totally understandable. Drawing attention to the child and pushing for involvement is not only disrespectful, it also may damage your relationship with that child forever. Instead, make the experience so much fun for the other children that reluctant children want to join in.

• **Try inviting reluctant children to lead the others in motions.** Kids leading motions don't necessarily have to sing; this may be just the spot a self-conscious child wants to find himself in. Again, don't force it; simply issue an invitation. You can also try moving beside the reluctant kids and singing or moving with them.

• **Above all, *don't draw unnecessary attention to the reluctant kids.*** If they fail to participate in singing but dive wholeheartedly into games that reinforce the Bible lesson or into other activities, they're still learning. Never assume that a lack of enthusiasm for your music time reflects personally on your abilities. It may be a reflection of how God has wired specific children to learn.

Children have favorite songs too. Be sure to incorporate a mix of "old favorites" and new songs so that children have some input into the music time too. And be sure that every song isn't one that's new. It takes considerable energy to teach a song and just as much energy to learn it; few children want to spend twenty minutes mastering new songs.

Have some new songs to teach? Here are some suggestions:

• **Start with the chorus.** The chorus may be the only part of the song kids learn initially, and in the case of some popular songs (Rich Mullins' "Awesome God," for instance), the chorus may be the only part of the song that is usually sung.

• **If children can read, have the lyrics on PowerPoint or transparencies.** A word of caution: Always respect copyright considerations. Making illegal copies of music or lyrics is just that: illegal. And doing so provides a poor example for children in your ministry.

• **Teach the song in child-sized bites.** After children master the chorus, sing the verse and let them sing both the chorus and verse. With some songs, that may be enough to teach children. In other situations there may be multiple verses you want children to learn. In that case, build on what children already know. And remember that repetition is helpful.

• **Limit the number of new songs, even if they're wonderful songs.** It's *work* to learn new music and lyrics, and worship time shouldn't be hard work for children. Plus, when we're focusing on learning new material, it's hard to focus on God. Be careful to not overwhelm children with new things to learn.

And here are answers to two questions I often hear when I'm leading workshops for children's music leaders:

• What if a parent doesn't approve of the music style I'm using?

It happens. Music is very personal, and while one parent might find it offensive to add too much beat to a song, another parent might object if a song is too "bland."

Don't feel pressured to quickly change your musical selections. Listen to parents' concerns and explain that you use a wide range or variety of music styles. Communicate both in words and actions that you value parents' concerns and suggestions.

Explain the lyrics of songs that parents find questionable and your reason for incorporating the song. More often than not parents reconsider their objections when they learn the lyrics and your objective for including the song.

• Why can't I just use any music I want to use, so long as it's for ministry?

Most Christian artists are active in local churches. They understand the need for music resources to be reasonably priced and easily available.

What some children's ministry leaders fail to understand is that when they photocopy copyrighted music scores or copy copyrighted tapes or CDs, those leaders are literally stealing the earnings due artists and music companies.

It's not only illegal to make copies of copyrighted material, it's also unethical. And it's unnecessary. Christian Copyright Licensing International (www.ccli.com) provides a way for churches to affordably and legally copy music for congregational use. It's surprisingly inexpensive, and it lets you project music on the screen with a clear conscience. The license you get from CCLI will answer questions you might have about making copies of tapes and CDs.

eleven

Puppets and Presentations That Connect With Kids

by Dale and Liz VonSeggen

The key to working with children is *variety*. Any good teaching method can become routine if overworked. Therefore, you must always look for creative ways to teach children.

Using a variety of teaching methods adds an element of surprise to your children's ministry. Children become more interested because you aren't predictable. They don't know what might happen next.

But don't let being original and varied keep you from covering the same concept more than once. Repetition is important to help kids learn. If you want children to learn that Jesus loves them, for example, teach it over and over again by using music, a story, an object lesson, a game, and a role-play—all in one lesson!

How can you creatively present information to children? Your creativity and resources are your only limitations, but here's help with five proven approaches: puppets, storytelling, clowning, drama, and illusions.

Puppets With a Purpose

Here's one reason to thank God for the invention of television: It has trained young children to appreciate puppets. Of course, *Sesame Street* and its kin have a level of production expertise you're unlikely to reach, but at least the concept holds: Kids like puppets. A hand puppet with a moving mouth can be a dynamic teaching tool.

You don't need a lot of expertise to use puppets. You can start by buying a commercially made puppet and simply letting the

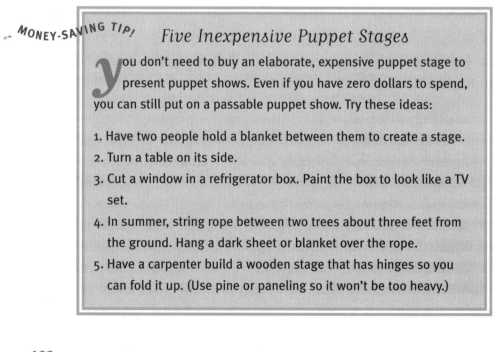

MONEY-SAVING TIP! *Five Inexpensive Puppet Stages*

You don't need to buy an elaborate, expensive puppet stage to present puppet shows. Even if you have zero dollars to spend, you can still put on a passable puppet show. Try these ideas:

1. Have two people hold a blanket between them to create a stage.
2. Turn a table on its side.
3. Cut a window in a refrigerator box. Paint the box to look like a TV set.
4. In summer, string rope between two trees about three feet from the ground. Hang a dark sheet or blanket over the rope.
5. Have a carpenter build a wooden stage that has hinges so you can fold it up. (Use pine or paneling so it won't be too heavy.)

puppet lip-sync to a song played on a nearby CD player. As you gain experience, you'll soon be writing your own scripts and creating different voices.

But whether you're a veteran puppeteer or a first-timer, it's important to know the basics:

- Open the puppet's mouth once for each syllable spoken.
- Be sure the eyes of the puppet look at the audience.
- Make sure the audience can see the puppet's body, arms, and head.

In addition to knowing the basics of operating puppets, it's important to gear puppetry to your audience's age. Some approaches that work well with older children fall flat with young children, and vice versa. We've found the following methods to be effective for the different ages:

Preschoolers—With preschoolers, use soft, touchable puppets to assist you as another voice in the classroom. It's amazing how much more attentive preschoolers are when a teacher says something and a friendly puppet agrees. Create a personality for the puppet that differs from your own. If possible, give the puppet a voice that children will enjoy hearing.

For preschoolers, action and repetition are more important than clever, funny scripts. Adapt nursery rhymes or familiar tunes for the puppet to use in teaching children some basic lessons.

For example, we've created various messages to the tune of "The Farmer in the Dell." One message that works with the tune is "I like you. I like you. I want a lot of friends, so I like you!" Another message: "Roses are red. Daisies are white. Let's take turns and never fight!" Or sing, "Roses are red. Grass is green. It is not nice to hit or be mean."

One Christmas we had three- and four-year-olds each make lambs by stuffing a lunch sack with newspaper, closing the end with a rubber band, and covering the bag with cotton balls. We also used medium-size sacks with one side cut out to make shepherds' headpieces for children to wear.

The children walked around the room carrying their lambs, searching for green pasture. When they got to a predetermined spot, an angel puppet appeared over the side of a "hill" and told them all about the baby Jesus born in Bethlehem. The children sure remembered that story!

Other ways to use puppets with preschoolers include:

• Use knock-knock or other simple jokes.

• Have puppets ask children yes-and-no questions.

• Have children clap or raise their hands if they hear the puppet make a mistake when saying a Bible verse or singing a song they know.

• Invite preschoolers to sing along with the puppet or sing a song *for* the puppet.

Kindergarten–Grade 3—With this age group, use a puppet as a guest in your classroom. Dress the puppet as a Bible character or visitor from another country. Have the children ask the puppet questions. Or consider having your children tell a puppet that always shows up late for class what Bible story the puppet missed.

Consider using a puppet to help with discipline. When discipline problems occur, have the puppet tell the children what went wrong. If done sensitively, the puppet's rapport with the children allows it to address the issue more freely without hurting feelings.

CREATIVE IDEA!

Storing Puppets

t ake advantage of discarded hat boxes, bags, a file cabinet, or another container to house your puppets so that children can't see or play with the puppets until you're ready to use them.

A puppet can be a great storyteller or contribute to the story the teacher tells. The puppet is fun and colorful to watch, and the puppet can confirm lesson truths for children.

Children at this age also enjoy repeating their memory work for a special puppet. Think about having a professor puppet or a wise owl on hand for children to recite to.

Grades 4–6—With older children, use puppets to play games. For example, play Twenty Questions with a puppet. This game lets children ask twenty yes-or-no questions, with the goal of figuring out the person, place, or event the puppet has chosen. The child who guesses the correct answer becomes the next puppeteer.

Have a puppet comment on how kids are doing at a craft or project. Or have a puppet that is a "cool" musician, disc jockey, guitar player, or drummer lead singing.

Children at this age can also make puppets and write their own scripts. Have them present puppet shows to younger children in your church.

Secrets of Successful Storytelling

Jesus often taught by telling stories. And when we read the parables he shared, it seems as if nothing could be easier than telling a story to help listeners discover a profound spiritual truth.

If only it were that simple.

Storytelling takes practice, especially if you'll be telling stories to children. Why? Because they're story *experts*, having heard hundreds. To connect with children, you need to be prepared. Here are some tips to get you ready.

• **Maintain eye contact**—Look directly into the eyes of your audience. Make people feel that you understand what they're thinking as you tell the story.

• **Paint word pictures**—Let your listeners visualize the characters by the way you describe them. If possible, show drawings or visuals. Children remember better when they hear *and* see a story.

• **Use sound effects**—Children love to hear how various characters sound. Practice creating several character voices. Make the sound of the wind or the sea or animals. Actually cry, yell, sneeze, or stutter if it adds to the story. You'll capture kids' attention, especially with very young children.

• **Incorporate variety**—Speak softly at times, then loudly, depending on what's happening in the story. Pause for suspense or surprise. When the action becomes exciting, talk more rapidly. When emphasizing a lesson at the end of the story, present it slowly. Consider repeating it.

How to Use Storytelling With Different Age Groups

Preschoolers—When telling stories to preschoolers, use large picture books so that children can see what's happening as you tell the story.

MONEY-SAVING TIP! *Transform Junk Into Storytelling Props*

isuals that appear in teacher guides or teaching visual-aid kits can be made into stand-up characters for storytelling. Simply tape the two-dimensional figures to something you usually throw away: empty toilet paper or paper towel tubes. Have the "tube" people in the story move and interact with other characters. After telling the story, give the characters to the children to use as *they* retell the story.

Visuals are crucial for preschoolers. If you don't have a picture book to tell a story, make visual story cards with bright colors. Have preschoolers actually participate in the story.

For example, in telling the story of feeding the five thousand, have children walk in place as if they were going to the mountainside. Next, describe how people felt when they saw Jesus. Have the children jump up and down because they're so happy. Then have preschoolers sit to listen.

During the story, have preschoolers act out getting sleepy by lying down and closing their eyes. Further on during the story, have the children pretend to be hungry and rub their tummies. As you tell the story, lead the motions.

In telling a story about Joseph, have children clap and smile when something good happens to Joseph. When something bad happens, have the children hold their heads in their hands, shake their heads, and say, "Oh, no!"

Kindergarten–Grade 3—Object lessons make for wonderful attention-getting stories for children of this age—*if* the lessons are concrete and easy to understand. Avoid object lessons that teach abstract concepts children won't understand.

For example, the biblical concept that we are "the salt of the earth" is too abstract for children of this age. Even sprinkling salt on a globe or having kids taste salt sprinkled into their palms won't make this concept clear. Their concrete mental capacities will still lead them to questions such as, "How can I get into a salt shaker?" Use age-appropriate concrete concepts such as God's love, forgiveness, prayer, or gifts.

Children at this age love having stories read to them. Use short children's books, or check out the stories written for children in devotional books for families.

Have children participate in stories. At this age, they can do more sophisticated actions than preschoolers. For example, consider using mops and brooms made into stick puppets. As you tell the story, some children move the puppets while other children do sound effects as you cue them.

Grades 4–6—Use Bible Charades to involve fourth- to sixth-graders in your story. Provide ideas and props for one or two children to silently act out a story while the rest of the group guesses who the characters are and what's happening in the story.

Some good Scripture stories for children to act out include:

• 1 Samuel 16:1-13, where David is chosen to be king after Saul;

• 1 Kings 17, where the widow of Zarephath gives away her last bit of food;

• Luke 5:1-9, where Peter's obedience to Jesus results in catching lots of fish; and

• Acts 16:16-34, where Paul and Silas, jailed for preaching about Jesus, win the jailer to Christ.

Object lessons work well with this age group. In fact, children at this age enjoy being given an object and making up their own lesson. Tap their creativity! Start with the object and ask children to use it in a story from the Bible, or start with a story and ask children to incorporate objects as props as you tell the story.

These children are particularly interested in object lessons with surprise endings or ones that have a chemical reaction or optical illusion. It's important, though, to keep the object lessons sufficiently concrete and specific.

You can also involve children in stories by having them illustrate a story with chalk or markers as you tell it. Have children all do this at the same time, or have one child draw in front of the group on a flip chart or blackboard. Children love to watch a peer draw.

Ministering With Clowns

Clowns make children laugh, smile, and snicker. Clowns can captivate a child without saying a word. And a clown can teach a lesson a child will long remember.

Clowning involves more than pulling on floppy shoes and a red nose. You must also develop a personality and purpose for your character. A clown performing in the context of children's ministry needs to demonstrate a childlike faith and act with Godlike acceptance of everyone. This character should give away love and share joy when interacting with children.

If you choose to use clowns in your ministry, be sensitive to the developmental differences of children of different ages.

Preschoolers—Maintain a distance from young children, and gesture your greeting. If you see a favorable response, you may move closer, but be prepared to move away if your clown frightens a child. Preschool children often fear a white-faced or highly animated clown.

Don't think you always have to wear the entire clowning garb with children this age. Consider doing a skit with just a clown hat or red nose. Large clown props such as a comb, toothbrush, or fluffy bath towel work well to capture preschoolers' attention.

Kindergarten–Grade 3—Clowns make good greeters to shake

hands or pat children's heads as children enter class. Have a clown create interest in a subject. For example, give the clown a treasure chest labeled "World's Greatest Treasure." As a child comes close to peek, have the clown open the lid to show a picture of Jesus inside.

Children at this age may enjoy face painting. Paint different faces that reflect different moods, such as happiness, sadness, worry, or fear. Have an entire group of children express actions and show feelings with their faces and bodies as you tell a story.

Children this age also love parades. Create a parade of children with clowns to promote an upcoming event such as vacation Bible school. Have children parade into a worship service with the clowns to make an announcement. Or have children parade through a neighborhood, local mall, or your church's Sunday school classes.

Grades 4–6—By the time children are this age, they enjoy watching clown skits, but usually only if they don't have to become too involved in the skits.

Upper elementary children may antagonize a clown by stepping on his toes, pulling his nose, or stealing his props. A clown must be prepared with clever visual tools such as visual illusions.

And remember that no matter how many times his or her nose gets tweaked, a clown doesn't retaliate in kind!

Sixth-graders may enjoy becoming part of a clown ministry team. If you have interested kids, teach them how to correctly put on clown makeup, to develop a clown character, and to do skits to be presented to their peers or younger children.

A team of sixth-grade clowns can also provide an important ministry by visiting children in the hospital. Have clowns minister by waving, blowing kisses, and giving away cheery get-well cards. Or have clowns visit local retirement communities or nursing homes.

How to Use Drama to Communicate With Children

Bible dramas are a powerful tool for learning because children can more easily identify with people on stage than with people described in a book. Drama has many forms, from simple role-plays to full-scale dramatic productions that include memorizing scripts, wearing costumes, and building sets.

Use drama in different ways, depending on the age of the children in your ministry.

Preschoolers—Dramas with three- to five-year-olds should be simple, simple, *simple*. Have preschoolers wave palm branches while singing about Palm Sunday or pretend they're fishermen while you tell the story about Jesus telling Peter where to catch fish. Children can pretend to throw nets into the sea and pull out fish.

Preschoolers also enjoy simple role-plays, as long as they can act and not speak (although some young children are *very* willing to do sound effects). For example, as you tell the parable of the sower, have preschoolers act like farmers with bags of seeds on their shoulders. Have children walk in a straight line, pretending to plant seeds along a row as they walk.

Another way to use drama with preschoolers is to have them be "still" actors in a larger dramatic presentation that includes older children. Have preschoolers wear costumes, and give them poses to act in the "frozen picture." The nativity scene works well with preschoolers.

Kindergarten–Grade 3—Bible pantomimes are a fun way for children of this age to present a lesson to the class. Give one or two props to children doing the pantomime. Suggest several gestures or actions you want them to present. Encourage children to exaggerate the actions so that their peers can more easily guess the characters they're pantomiming and what the story is about.

Children at this age can be creative at role-playing. Assign each child a definite character. Explain how the story begins and ends, and let the children create what the characters say. It might be helpful to read aloud the Bible story before the children act it out.

Interviews are another type of dramatization, but you need to give children at this age lots of guidance. Provide questions and answers for those taking part. For example, one child may dress up as Paul. Children can ask "Paul" questions (which Paul would already have answers for). When children enjoy this type of dramatization, they eventually feel more comfortable ad-libbing the parts.

Grades 4–6—Older children enjoy the dramatization technique known as readers' theater. The teacher prepares a script ahead of time with narrator and actor parts. The children use only their voices to act. They may speak slowly, quickly, loudly, or softly, and use their voices in other ways. Several actors may speak lines together. The actors stand in a row at the front of the room or sit on stools. Whenever a child appears in a scene, he or she faces the audience. In a scene where the child isn't present, he or she faces away from the audience.

Fourth- to sixth-graders are quite good at mimicking well-known characters such as reporters and famous people. After presenting a lesson, ask children to write a few sentences to summarize the lesson and then present the information as if they were famous people, such as the president, a reporter, a movie star, or a singer.

Don't overlook full-scale plays or musicals. These require a lot of work, but some children really enjoy them. Have kids make props and scenery, prepare posters, design the program, sing, act, or make costumes. Such an activity can benefit not only your audience but also the children involved. Full-scale dramas can build community in your group.

Illusions: Memorable Presentations

In some circles, the term *magic* is associated with the occult. However, there's nothing wrong with the element of surprise or the unexpected. Jesus did the unexpected when he told Peter to catch a fish. Of course, this wasn't magic, but a miracle. And while we can't perform miracles like Jesus did, we can create illusions to demonstrate Bible truths.

Over the years children have enjoyed lessons we've presented using chemical reactions to demonstrate truths. For example, one tablespoon of white vinegar mixed in three tablespoons of water will bubble up and foam over the edge of a glass when you stir a teaspoonful of baking soda into the water. The same soda stirred into plain water will not react. We use this illusion to demonstrate that we can't see sin inside a person, but when a person acts on the sin, everyone can see it.

Daring to Be Creative

This chapter has presented only a few ideas about how to make creative presentations to children. They'll hopefully get you started thinking about new ways to teach children.

Being creative isn't enough. You also need to be *daring*. Daring enough to try something new—something outside your comfort zone. Use common objects in uncommon ways. Jesus used a boy's lunch and a fig tree to teach important lessons.

And be brave. Look for new ways to teach children. Dress up a broom as a Bible character to talk to your class. Have children present a story using balloons they've decorated as people. The possibilities are endless.

And the possibilities will make learning a lot more fun and memorable for children.

Planning a Creative Presentation

BEFORE THE PRESENTATION

Lesson topic:

Scripture:

Creative techniques you plan to use:

Materials required:

Senses the creative presentation will include:

____Sight ____ Sound ____ Smell ____ Taste ____ Touch

Time needed for presentation:

AFTER THE PRESENTATION

Actual time used:

Children's attention: *Excellent   Good   Fair   Poor*

Children's comments:

Spontaneous additions that occurred during the presentation:

Suggestions for improvement:

Where presentation materials are stored:

*part*3
Age-Specific
Ministries

twelve
Nursery Notes

by Jean Cozby

Your family is new in town, and you're visiting churches. You enter a church building, and you're greeted warmly as you're handed a bulletin. In response to your question about the nursery, you're directed down a hallway to your left.

And that's when you decide that this isn't the church for your family.

Why?

Because no matter how wonderful the sermons, how worshipful the music, and how focused the prayer, you won't leave your eighteen-month-old daughter in a dimly lighted room cluttered with outdated cribs and unsafe toys.

A nursery fitting that description almost screams, "WE

DON'T CARE ABOUT CHILDREN!"

Want to make a good first impression on visitors with young children? Start in the nursery.

How to Teach Babies and Toddlers About God

Infants as young as four to six months old respond to happy times at church. By nine months, infants who've received loving care from parents and caregivers who talk to them regularly about God may begin to associate God and Jesus with good feelings.

And simple Bible thoughts, stories, and concepts aren't beyond the reach of toddlers.

Teaching techniques to use in your nursery include:

Bible conversation—As nursery workers talk with and hold babies, have them include statements such as "Adrienne is a pretty baby. God made Adrienne so special."

Music—Singing to children doesn't require professional talent! Music soothes crying infants, lulls tired babies to sleep, and delights active toddlers. Select simple songs that use the name of Jesus.

Manipulatives—any child-safe objects that babies can touch can serve as teaching tools. Simply tell children that God made things soft...or hard...or yellow...or green.

Prayer—It's never too soon to begin praying for children. When you pray with babies and toddlers, use simple words they can understand. Refer to God as "God" rather than "Lord" or "Father." Using other names will confuse babies who are only just beginning to understand that God is a person.

What happens in your nursery will give infants and toddlers a solid foundation for their Christian faith, as well as allow their parents to be part of your church's ministry. And the patient, loving care you provide is an encouragement to parents as they raise their children at home.

Start Here: Church Nursery Essentials

Here are five keys to making your nursery safe and effective.

• **Cleanliness**—Regularly clean your nursery. Since babies put everything in their mouths, clean all toys and surfaces with a mild disinfectant each time the room is used.

Wash all sheets, blankets, and other washable items after each individual use. Put wax paper on changing tables to keep germs from spreading. Toss out the wax paper after babies leave.

You'll have a lot of laundry to do, but dividing the task between volunteers lessens the load.

Require volunteers to wear aprons since babies spit up and spill things. And have nursery workers remove their shoes. This eliminates the dirt that adults track onto carpeted areas and protects little fingers and toes from dangerous heels.

And be sure to check and carefully control the nursery's lighting, ventilation, and temperature control.

• **Safety**—Require at least one person with CPR and first-aid training to be in the nursery when children are present. Post emergency numbers, such as your local hospital and poison-control office. Also, have parents fill out a form listing their child's allergies, the child's exact age, and snacks the child should or shouldn't have. Update forms frequently.

Ask parents where they'll be during nursery hours and where they usually sit. You want to be able to find parents quickly and easily.

For a top-to-bottom evaluation of your nursery, refer to the chart on page 142.

• **Supervision**—Provide adequate supervision. Parents will feel more comfortable leaving children in the nursery when their children receive individual attention, and you'll provide better care for children.

How many nursery workers are enough? Check with your local licensing agencies to get information about child-to-staff ratios, and meet or exceed those standards. Your children deserve it.

Have enough volunteers on hand so that each child is greeted individually as he or she comes into the room. And make sure each child's belongings are labeled and stored properly.

• **Security**—The larger your church grows, the less likely it is that your nursery staff will know every parent and child. Develop a way to guarantee that a child won't be taken by a stranger or a noncustodial parent. Some churches make do with sign-in and sign-out sheets. Others use a wristband system. Whatever system you put in place, don't make exceptions.

• **Discipline**—Volunteers often express frustration about what they can and can't do when disciplining toddlers. And because inappropriate discipline can be so damaging to everyone involved, it's important that you provide thorough training to all volunteers.

Be certain that when providing discipline, your volunteers let children know they're loved for who they are, not for how they act. And have no more than one or two rules for your classroom. Toddlers won't remember more, so a list of six or seven is a wasted effort. "Be kind to each other and our things" pretty well covers most situations that arise.

Establish and communicate your discipline policy to staff, volunteers, and parents. There shouldn't be any surprises, and having an established policy helps if tempers begin to rise.

Training Tips for Nursery Workers

The quality of care in your church nursery is directly related to the training you provide volunteers. Dependable, well-trained volunteers are a must.

Some churches require parents who use the nursery to take turns staffing it once per month or per quarter. Great idea, but be mindful that these occasional volunteers still must be trained.

Teenagers make great volunteers and have a wide variety of child-care skills. Set standards such as requiring teenagers to pass a Red Cross Babysitting Course and/or having significant experience with younger siblings.

Be aware that teenagers often get distracted and are very social. Be clear that if teenage friends serve together in the nursery,

Nursery Discipline in a Nutshell

*i*f a child in your nursery bites or hits another child, follow these steps immediately.

- Talk to the child. Tell the child how he or she hurt another child and that it's improper to do that. For example, say, "Jason, you bit Suzie and hurt her. She is crying. I wouldn't let Suzie bite you, and I'm not going to let you hurt her, either."

- Have one person watch the child for the rest of the session. It's OK for the child to know that he or she is being watched. Be ready to remove the child if another incident occurs.

- Tell the child's parent. Explain what happened and how you dealt with it. Ask the parent to also talk with the child at home about what happened and explain why the behavior was unacceptable.

- If the child repeats the incident the following week, immediately call the parent out of the worship service or class to remove the child from the nursery. Explain to the parent that this is the next step in your discipline policy.

Also explain to the child what's happening. For example, say, "Jason, your mom had to leave her Sunday school class to get you today because you hurt Suzie. Our rule is to be kind to each other and our things. We love you and want you in our nursery, but you can't come if you keep hurting people."

they need to be focused primarily on the infants and toddlers, not each other.

Design your training to be both instructive and encouraging. If your volunteers don't feel appreciated or affirmed, you're training people who will soon leave your ministry. Be intentional about supporting, equipping, *and* training your staff.

Some tips for making your training effective:

Stay focused. Your volunteer workers probably don't need to know about the latest trends in child development theory, but they *do* need to know what to do if one child bites another. Keep your training practical, relevant, and responsive to the needs of your staff.

Pick a good time for training. News flash: Nobody likes meetings. But if you've told people up front that training is part of their job description (see "Job descriptions" on page 52), they'll come—maybe. Remove as many obstacles as possible.

Provide mentoring. Especially for new staff and teenagers, you'll find that pairing up new volunteers with long-term volunteers is an effective way to get some "on the job" training.

Don't try to do it all yourself. Call your area hospital or Red Cross. See if you can take an existing course or join in training offered by area day-care centers.

Nursery Staffing Chart

ratios will vary depending on your location and individual situation, but here are some guidelines:

- **Infants:** two children per worker
- **Crawlers:** three children per worker
- **Toddlers:** four children per worker
- **Two-year-olds:** five children per worker

Floor-to-Ceiling Nursery Safety Checklist

FLOORS

☐ I have crawled around the room to survey it from a baby's perspective.

☐ I have removed any small objects that babies can pick up and put into their mouths.

☐ I have inspected the rugs to see that they have nonskid, nonstick backing. If they don't, I have removed or replaced them.

☐ I have cleaned all carpets, rugs, and floors.

WALLS

☐ I have confirmed that the walls are painted with lead-free paint.

☐ I have inspected the walls for peeling or chipped paint and have repainted or covered problem spots. (Large bulletin boards work great for this.)

☐ I have inspected the walls for loose or peeling wallpaper and have reattached or covered problem spots.

☐ I have cleaned all the walls.

FIRST AID

☐ I have placed a stocked first-aid kit out of children's reach.

☐ I have provided phone numbers for local poison control and hospital emergency rooms, and I have posted the location of the nearest telephone.

FIRE SAFETY

☐ I have installed and tested a smoke detector and a carbon monoxide detector.

☐ I have placed a fire extinguisher out of children's reach.

☐ I have provided a map to the nearest outside exit.

☐ I have routed electrical cords safely out of walking areas. (Walking on electrical cords, even if they're covered with rugs or carpeting, can break their wiring and cause fires.)

FURNITURE AND FIXTURES

☐ I have shielded old-style radiators to protect children from being burned.

☐ I have stored plastic bags, diaper-changing supplies, and cleaning supplies in latched cabinets or out of children's reach.   →

☐   I have covered all electrical outlets with safety plugs.

☐   I have removed all electrical cords from children's reach.

☐   I have anchored or secured all furniture and shelves to prevent children from pulling them over.

☐   I have placed foam or other padding on any sharp corners or edges.

☐   I have removed all poisonous plants and placed any nonpoisonous live plants out of children's reach.

☐   I have removed thumbtacks and staples from bulletin boards within children's reach.

☐   I have checked all cabinet and furniture knobs to see that they're securely fastened.

☐   I have removed any unnecessary furnishings or supplies from the room.

WINDOWS

☐   I have inspected windows and screens to ensure that they're securely fastened.

☐   I have moved furniture and equipment away from window areas.

☐   I have secured drapery or window-covering cords out of children's reach.

DOORS

☐   I have installed locks or latches on any doors that children can reach and possibly open.

☐   I have ensured that all doorstops have no removable parts.

CEILING

☐   I have inspected ceiling tiles to ensure they're firmly in place.

☐   I have removed, inspected, cleaned, and replaced all overhead lighting fixtures.

☐   I have inspected textured ceilings and removed any loose plaster.

After you've completed this checklist, file it for future reference—you may need it again. Or post it in or near your church nursery to let parents know that their children's safety is your first concern.

Adapted from *The Safe and Caring Nursery* by Jennifer Root Wilger. © 1998 Jennifer Root Wilger. Published by Group Publishing, Inc. Used by permission. For in-depth, practical help setting up or updating your church nursery, turn to *The Safe and Caring Nursery* for great advice!

When to Refuse Sick Children

It probably feels wrong to refuse to accept children into your church nursery, but when kids are sick, you really have no choice. You owe it to the other children to not expose them to the colds, flu, and other illness that babies and toddlers seem to collect so easily.

If a child with an obvious illness is presented to you at the nursery, gently explain that your policy won't allow you to accept visibly ill children. Most parents appreciate your protecting their children from similar exposure and will understand.

It helps if you have an established, written policy that you've already given to parents and posted prominently. Being proactive also helps you avoid unpleasant situations, because parents know what is and isn't acceptable.

If a child begins to show symptoms of illness while in your care, send for the child's parents as soon as possible. Have a space in your nursery where you can keep an apparently ill child until a parent arrives.

Opinions vary about what conditions should keep a child from entering a nursery, but these are generally accepted reasons:

- fever—currently or within the previous twenty-four hours;
- a runny nose with a colored discharge;
- pink eye (conjunctivitis) or other eye infections;
- flu or flu symptoms;
- a sore throat;
- vomiting within twenty-four hours;
- diarrhea within twenty-four hours;
- skin rashes or infection;
- strep throat (unless the child has been diagnosed and medicated for at least twenty-four hours);
- symptoms of measles, mumps, scarlet fever, chicken pox, or other childhood diseases; and
- head lice (no nits can remain).

thirteen

Discovering the World With Preschoolers

by Mary Irene Flanagan, C.S.J.

Plant a tiny acorn, and a mighty oak will grow— eventually. Preschoolers are like tiny acorns. As we help nurture their young faith, we have to wonder: Will these tiny acorns grow into mature believers? Will they pro- duce fruit for the kingdom? Will the seeds of faith we plant someday flourish and become mighty, towering testimonies to God's greatness?

Just as gardeners carefully prepare soil to receive a seed, so, too, must we prepare deeply impressionable preschoolers for a spiritual awakening.

Our preparation first requires that we live out the love of God in our relationships with preschoolers. Our actions, and the attitude with which we interact with preschoolers, carry far more weight than the words we say to them.

The second part of being prepared requires that we understand preschoolers and how they learn.

Understanding Preschoolers

If psychologists don't yet understand preschoolers, it isn't for a lack of effort.

Psychological research has stirred considerable interest in early childhood development. According to researchers such as Jean Piaget[1], Erik Erikson[2], Lawrence Kohlberg[3], and Rhoda Kellogg[4], physical, emotional, intellectual, social, and moral development follow an orderly, consistent, recognizable, and predictable pattern.

According to Piaget, preschoolers are in the pre-operational stage, which Mary Ellen Drushal, author of *On Tablets of Human Hearts*, breaks into two stages: pre-conceptual and intuitive.

During the pre-conceptual period, children age two to four are egocentric; they don't understand how another person feels. Two-to four-year-olds classify objects by a single characteristic, meaning

Getting to Know Your Preschoolers

reading about early childhood development will help you understand this age group better, but to do ministry most effectively, you'll need to spend individual time with each child to get to know him or her.

If at all possible, prearrange a forty-five-minute home visit. During this time, concentrate on getting to know the child. Go to the child's room. See the child's yard and play area. Meet the child's pets and stuffed animals. Find out what interests the child, and establish a relationship with the child and his or her family.

a rose is a rose and a daisy is a daisy. However, these children don't understand that both are flowers.

Around age four, children reach the intuitive period. At this stage children are still egocentric, but their intellectual capacity greatly expands. Children can use numbers (although they can't explain why), and they can classify things into groups. For example, children now understand that both a rose and a daisy are flowers.[5]

As preschoolers begin making these connections, they also begin forming a foundation for their faith. "The first seven years [of life] constitute the period for laying the foundations of religion," says R. S. Lee, the author of *Your Growing Children and Religion*. "This is the most important period in the whole of a person's life in determining his later religious attitudes."[6]

Clearly, your ministry to preschoolers is important!

How to Give Preschoolers a Spiritual Foundation

The goal of your preschool ministry shouldn't be to "give" young children religion. Preschoolers aren't developmentally ready for formal instruction in faith. They can't interpret Scripture, understand deep theological concepts, or participate meaningfully

---

Photogenic Walls

*h*elp young children "see" how they're important people in God's eyes. Ask parents to each bring a picture of their child. (Or you can have an instant-print camera ready and take pictures of children as they arrive.)

Label each picture with the child's name so parents and teachers can more easily learn all the children's names. Use children's names often and always in a loving tone.

---

in adult religious practices. Preschool programs that assume young children are ready for these things can actually do a great disservice to preschoolers.

Rather, the goal of your preschool program should be to provide experiences that encourage children to eventually develop a mature appreciation of the faith.

Your top priority, then, isn't to communicate religious information. It's to provide a healthy, loving, family environment. Doing so reinforces a preschooler's sense of trust and independence. It recognizes the child's need for self-awareness, self-confidence, self-expression, and self-appreciation. It provides a structure that successfully engages the child's developing initiative and inventiveness.

If preschoolers feel valued and accepted in your class, they'll want to return to experience more of these feelings. Eventually they'll want to learn about the *source* of these feelings. This becomes the foundation on which more mature faith understanding can be built.

Making God Real to Preschoolers

So how do we lead young children to discover a loving God?

The primary goal in preschool is to awaken children's friendly relationship with God. Later on, the children can more easily come to know God in the person of Jesus and in the Holy Spirit.

Because preschool children are self-centered, plan lessons that encourage young children to love themselves. Before children can love others, they must first love themselves.

But all your lessons shouldn't be geared for the self-centered nature of preschoolers. At this age, children are beginning to reach out to others. They need to experience lessons on family,

Evaluating Your Preschool Program Worksheet

*e*valuate the effectiveness of your preschool program by answering these questions:

QUESTIONS	YES	NO
1. Are your program's themes expressed in concrete ways preschoolers can understand and relate to?	❏	❏
2. Does your program avoid theological concepts and training that preschoolers can't understand?	❏	❏
3. Does your program promote creativity by encouraging each child's self-expression?	❏	❏
4. Does your program avoid pre-drawn art, which suggests comparisons and standards beyond the child's ability?	❏	❏
5. Does your program respect preschoolers' physical capabilities by not asking them to perform tasks beyond their abilities?	❏	❏
6. Does your program affirm self-worth by valuing and accepting each child's creative work?	❏	❏
7. Does your program provide creative activities that preschoolers can do on their own without an adult's direct intervention?	❏	❏
8. Does your program encourage parents to participate on a regular basis?	❏	❏
9. Does your program encourage parents to extend each lesson theme by giving parents additional resources for the home?	❏	❏

If you answered yes to each of the nine questions above, your program is on sound educational, psychological, and theological footing. You're providing an environment that encourages later faith development in your preschoolers.

friends, and community that encourage them to love others. If three- to five-year-olds don't love people they can see, how can we expect them to love God, who they can't see?

Young children, by nature, live in a world where there's a fine line between fantasy and reality. Therefore, ground lessons in the concrete by dealing with the child's world. Help children see that sand, dirt, plants, and animals are gifts from God.

For preschoolers, their faith experience is based on life experiences. God's revelation occurs in the world of bugs and hugs. However, children need to learn to *interpret* these works of God, which is where you fit in.

A preschooler's world is one of discovery. So when a four-year-old discovers ants, share in the excitement. Explain that God made the ants. By sharing in the discovery and wonder with a child, we begin to lay the foundation for faith. It's in those quiet moments of wonder when a little one says, "Wow!" that a child's prayer life begins. Make prayer natural and spontaneous, rather than forcing preschoolers to memorize formal, traditional prayers.

A Prayer Preschoolers Can See

Since preschoolers are visual and concrete, make prayer something they can see. Have each child cover a box or a plastic two-liter soft drink bottle with colorful magazine pictures of things that are important to them. For example, a four-year-old may paste pictures of a dog, a family, carrots, the sun, and a toy on the container.

After preschoolers finish their prayer containers, have one child pass around his or her container. Have children take turns holding the container and praising or thanking God for one thing pictured on it.

As preschoolers grow and develop, their first images of God come from their experiences with their parents. Preschoolers who have loving, caring parents can understand that God is loving and caring. Conversely, children living in difficult home situations may have trouble seeing God as loving. But that doesn't mean you should give up on these preschoolers! Your loving relationship with these children will help them see that God truly loves them.

Making Religious Holidays Meaningful

Three- to five-year-olds love holidays! But when we celebrate holidays, especially Christian holidays, we need to be careful what we emphasize.

At Christmas, giving minute details of Jesus' birth isn't helpful. Since young children slip in and out of a fantasy world, they become confused by too much detail. Children will understand these concepts when they're older. For example, a four-year-old will not understand the virgin birth. A child may end up thinking Mary had two husbands—Joseph and God!

Instead, emphasize the part of the Christmas story preschoolers can understand. Tell them God loves them so much that he gave us all a great gift: his own Son, Jesus. Talk about how happy Mary, his mother, was and how she loved and cared for Jesus.

In preparing Christmas celebrations, do learning experiences that let preschoolers experience the joy and happiness of this season. Explain that the holiday is a birthday celebration for someone special: Jesus. Give preschoolers the experience of anticipating a great birthday party, giving gifts, and having fun.

Easter is another significant holiday, but a difficult one for preschoolers to grasp. The Easter message of Jesus' resurrection goes far beyond what young children can comprehend.

Make Easter a concrete experience for preschoolers. Put up a full-size cross in the churchyard so preschoolers can see how big it is. Preschoolers can carefully touch nails and thorns to see how much they hurt.

It's tempting to use Easter eggs, bunnies, and chocolate chicks for children to experience Easter. However, there's danger in using a secular approach to Easter.

Instead, help preschoolers discover that Christ's death and resurrection really happened. Use examples of new life as signs of new life from God. For example, showing how a caterpillar spins a cocoon and then comes out as a butterfly is a good way to explain how Jesus died and rose again.

Learning by Experience

Preschoolers' lives are grounded in the world of here and now. They learn by doing, smelling, tasting, feeling, hearing, and seeing. They don't have a sense of history or the ability to understand the past. Therefore, concentrate on the concrete values presented in Scripture that preschoolers can understand and experience. They can understand the loving care of God as they love one another and praise and thank God. That is, preschoolers can understand these concepts as long as we give children a way to *experience* those concepts.

Active, hands-on learning lets preschoolers learn through their fingers, eyes, ears, noses, and even their taste buds. Your lessons become experiences they remember.

As you design age-appropriate lessons, you encourage your preschoolers to participate, explore, imagine, and express themselves. As you creatively create a joy-filled atmosphere and your loving attitude draws preschoolers to you, you do ministry that will shape young lives forever.

Endnotes

1. Jean Piaget and Barbel Inhelder, *The Psychology of the Child* (New York: Basic Books, 1969).
2. Erik H. Erikson, *The Life Cycle Completed: A Review* (New York: Norton, 1982).
3. Lawrence Kohlberg, "The Developmental Approach to Moral Education," *Moral Education: Interdisciplinary Approaches*, edited by C. Beck, B. Crittenden, and E. Sullivan (Toronto: Toronto Press, 1970).
4. Rhoda Kellogg, *The Psychology of Children's Art* (New York: CRM, Inc., 1967).
5. Mary Ellen Drushal, *On Tablets of Human Hearts* (Grand Rapids, MI: Zondervan, 1991) 54-55.
6. Mary Irene Flanagan, *Preschool Handbook* (New York: Harper & Row, 1990), 6.

fourteen

Elementary Children

by Vince Isner and Dan Wiard

Here's a statement that few will challenge: Children change *dramatically* during their elementary years.

Obvious, isn't it?

There's a *universe* of difference between kindergartners and sixth-graders: how they process information, their physical abilities and size, their energy levels, neurological differences, emotional differences. The list goes on and on.

When you consider all the variables, it's a wonder that children of different ages have *anything* in common. Yet in children's ministry we're committed to working with children of every age...and doing so effectively.

And often the front-line troops we send into the fray are

inexperienced teachers who aren't familiar with the unique characteristics of children in their classes. It can be a recipe for disaster.

A kindhearted teacher in a second-grade classroom who tries to launch a debate between premillennial and postmillennial advocates won't get much of a response. The same is true for a sixth-grade teacher who asks boys and girls to form a circle and hold hands.

This chapter is a crash course for you and your staff. You'll get a quick outline of what's age-appropriate for children age five through sixth grade, with two important qualifiers:

1. Two children who are the same age may be very different. One fifth-grader is advanced beyond her years academically, and her fifth-grade friend struggles to do third-grade math. Some sixth-grade girls look like eighth-graders, while some sixth-grade boys have barely begun to mature physically. Each child is a unique creation of God!

2. A child may be a second-grader in one way and a fourth-grader in another. Matt is a straight-A fourth-grader who's reading at a sixth-grade level. He has the social skills of a second-grader and physically resembles a third-grader. How old is he *really*?

So consider the generalizations that follow as just that: generalizations. You'll need to fine-tune what's most appropriate in your children's ministry as you consider the children God has sent you to serve.

And before you run out and recruit a teacher for each age level, consider multi-aging your classrooms.

Multi-Aging Classrooms

A multi-age classroom is one in which children of various ages are a part of the learning community. The approach was once standard procedure in small schools such as "one-room" schoolhouses.

The reason for multi-aging out on the frontier was simple:

There weren't enough children to have multiple classrooms. And even if there were enough children, there often weren't enough teachers!

This old-time approach to grouping students has enjoyed a revival in school classrooms—and for good reason.

Multi-age groups are "families" of learners. And just like in real families, older children help younger ones master new skills, learn by example, and practice what they're learning.

Older children enjoy being the "big kids," too, and having an opportunity to step into helping roles.

Some leaders find it's helpful to multi-age within designated age groupings, such as first- through third-graders and fourth- through sixth-graders. Depending on the number of children in your program and the expertise of your volunteers, this may be more beneficial than having a multi-age group include first- through sixth-graders.

Creating Classes by Skill-Level Grouping

One variation of multi-aging is to create multi-age groups of children who share a skill level. For example, you might place all children who are accomplished readers in one group for an activity, while also creating a group of children who are still sounding out letters.

Children's Developmental Stages and Needs

Here's a thumbnail sketch of what your volunteers can expect from younger and older elementary children you serve...

5-Year-Olds	Grades 1 & 2
PHYSICALLY	
• Are more coordinated, agile, and strong • Need lots of room to run, hop, jump, and move around • Develop hand skills; can cut large objects and almost color within the lines	• Enjoy active play such as jumping and running • Experience a slowing in rapid growth • Develop small muscle coordination; begin to write
EMOTIONALLY	
• Thrive on the attention of other peers and adults • Feel proud when praised for doing something well • Feel self-conscious when compared to other children	• Express feelings with physical action; may hit others • Crave attention • Are self-centered; each child wants to be first
SPIRITUALLY	
• Understand God made them • Articulate God's love by doing kind things to others • Notice when adults say one thing about God and then act differently	• Sense God's love and God's world by personal experience • Are baffled by the fact they can't see God • Don't comprehend the Bible's chronology except that the Old Testament came before Jesus and the New Testament talks about Jesus
SOCIALLY	
• Tattle to get attention • Prefer playing with two or three children instead of large groups • Want to play games other kids are playing or mimic activities that adults do	• Usually tolerate kids from different racial and economic backgrounds • Want to please teachers • Want to win and always be first
INTELLECTUALLY	
• Have an attention span of about five minutes • Can carry out instructions • Triple their vocabularies within one year	• Interested in concrete learning experiences such as dramatizations and rhythms • Can sit still for about six to seven minutes • Have a limited concept of time and space; are interested in the present, not in the past or future

GRADES 3 & 4	GRADES 5 & 6
PHYSICALLY	
• Develop speed and accuracy in playing games • Girls develop faster than boys, especially in small muscle skills • Play with lots of repetition to develop skills	• Grow in bone structure, making bones susceptible to injury • Differ in growth rates by gender; girls forge ahead of boys in height and weight; some girls may get their menstrual periods • Prefer same-sex activities since girls are developing faster than boys, and boys prefer to play rougher than girls
EMOTIONALLY	
• Easily become frustrated because of trying to do activities that are beyond them developmentally • Vent anger by teasing or criticizing others • Have difficulty accepting constructive criticism	• Are emotionally more balanced; tend to be more easygoing • Are becoming more self-conscious • Base feelings on how others respond to them
SPIRITUALLY	
• Want God's help and guidance • Want to become part of God's family but don't completely understand the concept of a personal savior • Question how God answers prayer	• Begin to understand biblical symbolism • Tell friends about God when excited about God • Want to attend church; want to do service projects
SOCIALLY	
• Want to fit in and belong to a peer group • Want to play with members of the same sex • Begin to be less dependent on adults	• Become interested in competition—but not in competition that points out the differences between them and their peers • Want peers to play fair; become upset when others break rules • Develop individual leadership qualities
INTELLECTUALLY	
• Can sit still for about eight to nine minutes • Can accurately group and classify information • Ask in-depth questions instead of simple questions	• Can usually sit still for ten to eleven minutes, although some children can become absorbed in a project that interests them • Can think *to* themselves, causing communication to drop off • Develop a wider range of interests

Key Developmental Differences Among Younger and Older Elementary Children

PHYSICAL

Young elementary children are highly energetic, and age-appropriate programming will take into consideration children's need to move and use their bodies to discover and experience the world around them.

Don't forget to include structured quiet time, too. Give young children time to reflect and think. One strategy for accomplishing this is to ask young elementary children to draw pictures of what they've learned. Talk with children about what they drew. You'll hear how your young children are interpreting what they've heard and have a chance to reinforce the lesson.

Older elementary children are approaching puberty, and their appearance is beginning to be important to them. They're maturing and have questions about their bodies.

Some girls at this age are beginning to develop breasts. Those with larger breasts may be the envy of the other girls and get the attention of the boys. Or these developing girls may feel like outcasts, since they don't look like their friends.

When working with older elementary children, here are some things to take into consideration:

• Intentionally build children's self-esteem. While this is important for younger elementary children, too, older elementary children are beginning to think abstractly, and as they realize others are looking at them, they often become self-conscious.

• Do one-to-one ministry, helping children who have difficulty integrating their physical changes into their lives and self-identities.

• Consider separating the sexes for any games or activities that require touching.

• Realize that both girls and boys may become awkward during growth spurts.

INTELLECTUAL

Younger elementary children often confuse cause and effect and may believe an angry wish might actually come true and hurt someone. By the time children are five or six, most of them begin to emerge from a world of make-believe and enter a more concrete world. They begin to look for things that are solid and dependable.

That "concrete" tends to be laws and rules. Children want to know what is and what isn't real. Is Santa Claus for real, or is he a hoax? Is it or is it not OK to swear, even if they hear their dads swear? For the most part, younger elementary children look for black-and-white answers. Things are either right or wrong, up or down, never in between.

And while younger elementary children don't always see *everything* quite so concretely, they do tend to look for categories in which to pigeonhole new information.

It's important that adult leaders be honest when children ask questions we don't have answers for. Children need to understand that some questions don't *have* answers or the answers haven't yet been made clear as God unfolds his plan for the universe and our lives.

Older elementary children are readier then their younger counterparts to make decisions and take initiative. They'll enthusiastically devote a lot of time to activities they enjoy, yet when something becomes boring, they're wiggling and squirming within minutes.

Their reading and writing skills are maturing, supporting new abilities to think abstractly and reason deductively. They sometimes challenge adult thinking. We need to respect their answers and thinking—sometimes they're right!

Fourth- to sixth-graders can question and evaluate different points of view. They can make personal decisions based on religious ideals and express their beliefs in more complex ways than younger elementary children. We need to provide opportunities for them to do just that.

Most significantly for their faith development, older elementary children can think abstractly. God no longer needs to be thought of in human form, as younger children often picture him. Love is a feeling, not a gift from Grandmother; and sorrow is an emotion, not the tears themselves. Older elementary children can begin to understand church doctrine.

EMOTIONAL

Young elementary children crave affirmation and attention. From parents, from peers, from teachers—for young elementary children, attention and affirmation are nearly on a par with oxygen. This is a need that will continue to be felt when they're older, but younger elementary children are often more open about their desire.

At the same time, some younger children lack the social skills to appropriately ask for the attention they want and need. Classroom discipline can be a challenge at this age (and almost every age!).

For older elementary children, being part of the group is a high priority. These children often bow to peer pressure, rather than stand up for what they believe. Because of this, helping children build supportive, open relationships with Christian peers and mentoring adults can be powerful. So can providing opportunities for children to apply Bible truths to their lives as they explore and anticipate decisions.

Older elementary children can easily become frustrated with themselves. They often compare themselves to their peers, and many feel they fail miserably. Offering opportunities for children to do significant service to others can help them feel useful.

And the world is changing.

In many key areas, elementary children have less control over their lives than in past generations. Although they enjoy more options for entertainment and pleasure, they often endure long, tightly scheduled days.

It's not unusual for children to be awakened at 6:30 a.m., rushed through dressing and gathering book bags, and then herded out the door to elementary school. They may gulp down toast or pastry in the minivan and wash down their breakfast with a thermos of milk.

After school, these children might board a van and be shuttled to a community center where they'll remain until 5:30 or 6:00 p.m. After eleven long hours, their parents pick them up, play with them for thirty minutes, and then begin the nightly bedtime routine.

Many adults live with a schedule like this and handle it well. But a schedule like this exerts extreme pressure on developing elementary children whose world is rapidly changing.

As children move from preschool to elementary school, the school (an outside clock) marks their time rather than their own internal clocks. Life becomes more competitive. Most children get graded for the first time. They begin to judge their own abilities. And if they try hard and fail, children at this age may conclude that they're not any good, and their self-esteem can plummet.

Don't let a kindergartner's or third-grader's cool and sophisticated veneer fool you. These children are still children and need to trade some of their hypercharged schedule for moments of childlike behavior.

No amount of enrichment activities, clubs, or even church programming can replace simple love and security. Children need time spent communicating with parents and significant adults who'll see, hear, accept, and invest in them on the child's behalf.

As you serve your children, include their families as well. Seek ways to encourage parents to step into primary roles in shaping their children's Christian faith through teaching and modeling.

And at all times, in all ways, share the love of God with the elementary children he has trusted to your ministry.

*a*s you consider how to best minister to elementary-age children, ask yourself these questions:

- **How well do we know our children?** What are their schedules? How far from where we meet do they live?

- **What is the purpose of our ministry?** What do we hope to accomplish? How does meeting those goals play out for different ages of children?

- **How involved are children's parents in our program?** our congregation? Do parents know what their children are doing in our program? Have we found a way to involve parents as leaders or partners? Do we send frequent personal notes and newsletters to children's homes?

- **How creative is our program?** Does it offer a variety of activities? Are children interested in these activities, or are kids bored?

- **How involved are children in shaping our ministry?** What ways do children have input in planning activities?

If you're attempting to shape and lead the ministry without an ongoing and personal knowledge of your children, you can expect to falter. But if you include children and their families in shaping the scope of your ministry, you'll see your children grow in their faith.

fifteen

Preteens

by Gordon and Becki West

Your preteen ministry begins with understanding preteens. If it's sometimes a struggle, know you're not alone. Many public schools and churches aren't sure what to make of preteens, either. Preteens are sometimes treated as either large children or very young teenagers. Neither approach addresses their unique developmental challenges and emerging social needs.

What *Is* a Preteen?

Preteens can be as young as nine or ten and as old as fourteen. "Preteen" is less of an age and more of a developmental stage. According to research done by Peter Scales of Search Institute, preteens are characterized by seven key developmental needs:

1. Positive social interaction with adults and peers
2. Structure and clear limits
3. Physical activity
4. Creative expression
5. Competence and achievement
6. Meaningful participation in families, schools, and communities
7. Opportunities for self-definition[1]

A successful preteen ministry program addresses these key needs and takes into consideration the physical, social, intellectual, and spiritual characteristics that describe preteen students.

How Effective Is Your Ministry to Preteens?

before making changes, it helps to determine how you're currently doing. Here are three quick ways to rate your effectiveness.

Ask your kids.

Ask the kids who attend—and who don't attend—what they think of the current programming. And find out how many of your kids have brought their friends for a meeting.

Ask your parents.

Ask parents what they wish your programming provided for their children, how well your programming is meeting their expectations, and how they'd like to help your programming change.

Run the numbers.

Are you growing? Increasing attendance doesn't tell the whole story, but it gives you insight into whether your programming ranks high with your kids.

Characteristics of Preteens

Physically, the rate of growth and change in preteens varies widely. Growth comes in spurts, causing preteens to sometimes be awkward and clumsy. Many preteens experience fatigue as their bodies work overtime to grow and change. They may crave sleep and sometimes find it all they can do to simply stay awake.

Because early adolescents are very physical, they like to be active and move about constantly. It's hard for them to sit still for long periods, even during your most compelling Sunday school lesson.

Emotionally, preteens are subject to dramatic mood swings. They're literally bombarded with hormonal changes as the onset of puberty releases a flood of hormones into their bodies.

It's important to remember that many preteens have little control over their emotions. With effort preteens *can* control their words and actions, but you'll need to be patient and model the behavior you want your preteens to consider appropriate.

Preteens may often be angry and quick-tempered. This anger comes from a variety of sources, including fatigue and feelings of inadequacy, rejection, or uncertainty. Preteens are often fearful and threatened by competition.

Preteens are riding a roller coaster of emotions and need your encouragement, support, and unconditional love. Your frequent, strong affirmations will reassure your preteens that you love and accept them, just as they are.

Socially, preteens find peers to be *incredibly* influential. As kids begin to break away from their families and express individuality and independence, they typically reach out to surrogate families to fill the void. A church youth group, class, or roster of buddies can fill this role.

You can't overestimate the power of providing a safe social environment for your preteens.

Preteens are self-critical and critical of others. Because of these tendencies, you can have a significant impact if you're accepting and nonjudgmental. And your ministry's appeal will rise if you provide carefully chosen activities at which your preteens can excel.

Intellectually, preteens are moving from concrete to abstract thinking, so even kids who have attended church for years may start to question their beliefs. Don't automatically assume it's your fault or even a bad thing; give preteens the space and information they need to understand and personalize their faith.

And though preteens' brains and neurological systems are almost fully developed, their practical experience is thin. That means you can't assume they'll solve adult problems in appropriate, mature ways. In spite of their assurances to the contrary, they still require guidance in making many adult decisions.

Spiritually, preteens are very open to a personal relationship with God. Their consciences are becoming more fine-tuned, especially about the behavior of others. For instance, your preteens will quickly point out when your behavior is inconsistent or you act in a way they consider unfair.

But don't expect preteens to necessarily apply the same standards to their own behavior. Preteens may condemn adults who cheat or steal, yet rationalize their own shoplifting or book report plagiarism.

Preteens: The Center of Their Own Universes

It's natural for preteens to be egocentric. It's just not always their most endearing characteristic.

Egocentrism is the inability to differentiate between our responses and the responses of those around us and between our thoughts and reality. And that pretty much sums up how some preteens interact with the world.

Preteens' brand of egocentrism tends to involve two mental

constructions: the "imaginary audience" and "personal fable."

• **Preteens create for themselves an imaginary audience.** They assume others are as obsessed with their behavior as they are. Sue might imagine that, because she bought new shoes, as she walks past a group of peers, they'll all notice and care about her shoes. Shawn may believe the zit forming on the end of his nose is as bright as a beacon to his friends.

This tendency to think everyone is focused on them makes preteens very self-conscious. No wonder preteens have difficulty staying plugged into church programs where they don't feel they belong.

Preteens may also be so self-absorbed that they don't offer others the same emotional support and positive feedback they desire to receive. As you work with preteens, you'll give more encouragement than you're likely to receive in return.

• **Preteens tell themselves a "personal fable."** Since preteens believe they're the center of attention, they believe their feelings and lives are special and unique. An early adolescent may tell himself that...

• his feelings are special and no one can feel what he feels;

• no one can understand him or his feelings;

• he's invincible, and he believes that bad things will only happen to others.

None of these portions of a personal fable are true, but they may inform you of how your preteens are living.

Given that preteens may find it difficult to concentrate on anyone but themselves, how do you minister to them? especially if they're not listening?

Make sure your ministry includes these fundamentals:

Opportunities for relationships. Even if they are uncertain about where they fit in the world, preteens want friendships with peers. Does your ministry provide adequate, noncompetitive opportunities to interact with others? If not, you'll find preteens quickly fade from sight.

Chances to shine. Does your ministry give kids a chance to use their abilities and gifts? a place to lead? a chance to contribute? Involving kids, especially in ways they feel good about, builds investment and commitment. And it provides places kids can connect with you and the ministry.

Significant opportunities to serve and stretch. Preteens are ready to take on significant projects and make significant contributions. Are they contributors to your ministry or just an audience? A good way to answer that question is to ponder this question: What if nobody showed up for a typical preteen program? Would that change what you do that day?

If you usually deliver a lecture or show a video, then your kids are pretty much an audience. If they failed to show up, you could still do the program.

But if you're actively discipling preteens by letting them plug into ministry and leadership opportunities, then your program would grind to a halt if kids failed to show up.

Your goal is to design programming that requires kids to be present, involved, and growing in their faith.

Knowing that your preteens will act like preteens and that it might be easier and quicker to do things yourself, still take the plunge of involving kids in significant ways. It will pay off as your preteens develop and mature.

Where Do Sixth-Graders Fit In?

Are they children or youth? Do they belong in the older elementary class or the youth meeting?

Churches typically handle sixth-graders in one of three ways:

• **The Traditional Method—sixth-graders in children's ministry.** The size of the group usually determines whether fifth- and sixth-graders are grouped together or sixth-graders have their own class.

• **The Middle School Method—sixth-graders in youth ministry.** With the rise of middle schools across the country, many churches have followed the trend. Sixth-graders meet with seventh-, eighth-, and perhaps ninth-graders.

• **The Transitional Year Method—sixth-graders are ministered to separately.** This gives sixth-graders the special attention they seem to need.

Most churches agree that the best grouping plan is to maintain consistency with local schools whenever possible. A caution: Wherever sixth-graders land on the organizational charts, a successful program *must* meet their developmental needs.

And if you choose to make changes in your church, proceed carefully. You'll discover there's loyalty to the way things have been done in the past.

Disciplining Preteens

The best way to handle discipline problems is by preventing problems from developing. Here are some strategies for heading off discipline problems.

• **Set clear boundaries.** Your preteens need and want boundaries. You can expect preteens to push against boundaries and test you. You'll pass the test when you firmly, fairly maintain the boundaries and communicate that you love your preteens.

• **Expect the best from your preteens.** You'll be surprised how often they rise to meet your expectations if you clearly communicate what you want.

• **Love your preteens unconditionally.** The consequence of loving your kids is that you'll design your ministry to meet *their* needs, not yours. The music may not be your favorite style or played at your favorite volume. Kids may insist on keeping their hats on, even during prayer. They may not care about all the things you think they should care about. But unconditional love sets the stage for your preteens to grow and mature.

• **Proactively develop positive relationships.** When preteens develop a positive relationship with an adult, their behavior improves. Once kids feel like their teacher is also a friend, the changes can be dramatic. Build relationships!

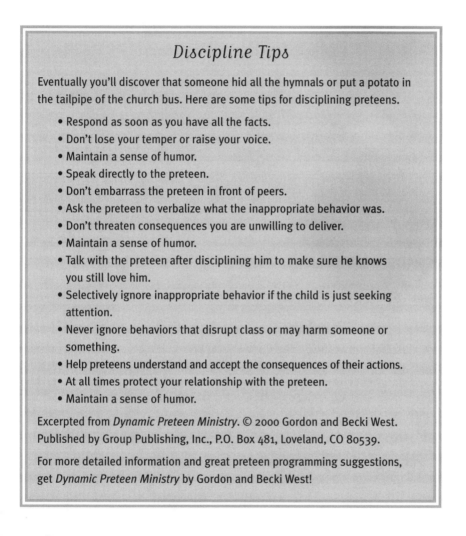

Discipline Tips

Eventually you'll discover that someone hid all the hymnals or put a potato in the tailpipe of the church bus. Here are some tips for disciplining preteens.

- Respond as soon as you have all the facts.
- Don't lose your temper or raise your voice.
- Maintain a sense of humor.
- Speak directly to the preteen.
- Don't embarrass the preteen in front of peers.
- Ask the preteen to verbalize what the inappropriate behavior was.
- Don't threaten consequences you are unwilling to deliver.
- Maintain a sense of humor.
- Talk with the preteen after disciplining him to make sure he knows you still love him.
- Selectively ignore inappropriate behavior if the child is just seeking attention.
- Never ignore behaviors that disrupt class or may harm someone or something.
- Help preteens understand and accept the consequences of their actions.
- At all times protect your relationship with the preteen.
- Maintain a sense of humor.

Excerpted from *Dynamic Preteen Ministry.* © 2000 Gordon and Becki West. Published by Group Publishing, Inc., P.O. Box 481, Loveland, CO 80539.

For more detailed information and great preteen programming suggestions, get *Dynamic Preteen Ministry* by Gordon and Becki West!

Endnote

1. Peter Scales, *Portrait of Young Adolescents in the 1990s* (Minneapolis, MN: Search Institute, 1991).

CHILDREN'S MINISTRY THAT WORKS!

part 4

Children's Ministry Programs

sixteen

Meaningful Programs for Children

by RaNae Street

Your children's ministry is much more than programs. And that's a good thing because programs don't change people; only *people* change people.

And yet your children's ministry includes programs. Lots of programs. The question is "Are they meaningful for your children and volunteers?"

What Makes a Program Meaningful?

It's not the quantity of programs that counts in children's ministry; it's how effective each program is in carrying out your church's mission and vision. Our goal is for every program we host to help connect children and their families with our church. We want to form a healthy relationship with children. It's that relationship that prompts kids and their families to come back.

It's important to pause and evaluate the strengths and weaknesses of your existing programs. Are they meaningful for children? How can you really know?

Here's an easy way to measure how likely a program is to be meaningful and life-changing: Ask if the "Four R's" are present in the program. If you see that a program is Relevant, Radical, Reflective, and Relational, you have a great program.

Here's what those words mean to me…

• **Relevant**—Make sure your programming is relevant to kids in your church *and* kids in your community. Take time to research kids' interests. Identify the specific needs of your church, area schools, and the families in your neighborhood. Every community is different, so avoid the temptation to simply import a program that's been successfully done elsewhere.

Don't rely on written surveys. Instead, make personal contact and actually *ask* what programming would be relevant. Pay attention to what resources are currently available. Prioritize program ideas so that you're meeting felt needs first.

• **Radical**—Churches lose their effectiveness when they try to offer programming that meets *all* the needs of children, their families, and their communities. Instead of trying to do it all and failing, focus on creating a program that's unique to your children's ministry. Intentionally select the "one thing" that will set your children's ministry apart from other churches in your area, then do it very, very well.

You won't be shortchanging your kids or their families, because you can refer families to capable, Christ-centered, community-based resources that your church simply can't provide.

The challenge is that to do one thing well, you may have to

stop doing several things poorly. There's a cost when you ask your church to stop doing programs that have outlived their effectiveness, but it's a cost worth paying if you can redirect resources to support truly meaningful programs. "The way we've always done it" may no longer meet the needs of your children.

• **Reflective**—Children love things that are exciting and fun, and meaningful children's ministries reflect excitement and fun. Meaningful programs are active, carefree, enthusiastic, inspiring, and unconcerned about failures. They reflect what children love to do, mirroring children's creativity and enthusiasm for hands-on learning. Meaningful programs also reflect real day-to-day situations that kids encounter, helping children apply what they're learning to those situations. Most importantly, meaningful programs reflect God's unconditional love and acceptance.

• **Relational**—Of the four common characteristics, *relational* is the most vital. Too often we focus on giving information, not transforming lives. Meaningful programs aren't focused on tasks. Rather, they facilitate an environment in which relationships can be built.

Relationships matter! We need to help children make new friends and help families build a network with other families and church leaders. Jesus' ministry is a great example of the importance of relationships. Jesus nurtured others through compassion and invested deeply in people who later changed the world. Our programs need to be places where children are turned on to faith through the power of relationships.

Meaningful Programs

At the heart of most children's ministries are Sunday school and midweek programs. Many churches focus nearly all their attention and finances solely on these two programs. But are these two programs enough?

Below are four different children's ministry program options. Each is designed to meet a different purpose, and each is important. A well-rounded, meaningful children's ministry includes each of these program options. Why? The goal is to engage a child at any point (probably at the outer ring of the target) and move that child toward the center of the target.

• **Momentum Programs**—These programs are designed to bring new people into the faith community. They're "come and see" events that provide positive first impressions of your ministry. Think of them as entry-level opportunities that facilitate numerical growth. Momentum events include theme days, special events, and community outreach events.

—Theme days promote excitement among children who are already part of your ministry and encourage children to invite friends. With a bit of creativity, you can turn nearly any day or event into a theme day. A few ideas to get you thinking are included in the chart on page 178.

—Special events are often seasonal and held once a year. Involved families are encouraged to invite their friends to join them for fun. Special events offer child-friendly activities and food. Make sure there's time for families who attend to get to know each other better.

—Community outreach programs are designed to fill a need or

interest in the community. They provide a partnership between the community and your church. Outreach programs offer families that aren't drawn by traditional Sunday school and church the chance to be exposed to spiritual people and biblical lessons.

A word of caution: Hosting a poorly executed event is worse than not hosting one at all, so plan for excellence.

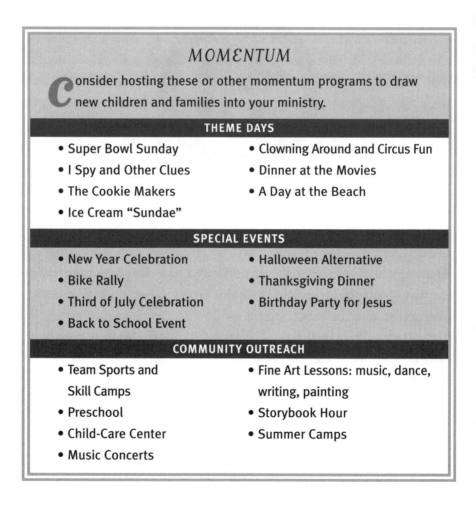

MOMENTUM

Consider hosting these or other momentum programs to draw new children and families into your ministry.

THEME DAYS

- Super Bowl Sunday
- Clowning Around and Circus Fun
- I Spy and Other Clues
- Dinner at the Movies
- The Cookie Makers
- A Day at the Beach
- Ice Cream "Sundae"

SPECIAL EVENTS

- New Year Celebration
- Halloween Alternative
- Bike Rally
- Thanksgiving Dinner
- Third of July Celebration
- Birthday Party for Jesus
- Back to School Event

COMMUNITY OUTREACH

- Team Sports and Skill Camps
- Fine Art Lessons: music, dance, writing, painting
- Preschool
- Storybook Hour
- Child-Care Center
- Summer Camps
- Music Concerts

• **Support Programs**—These programs offer assistance to families and children who are dealing with challenges. Support programs provide a safe place for children to learn, talk, and express their feelings.

Many support programs are offered as short-term classes or small groups that last between six and eight weeks. The goal is to help kids explore issues in the context of the guidance found in God's Word. Support programs offer more than just coping skills; they also provide hope.

Be certain you have leaders for these programs who are adequately trained and who love and serve God.

SUPPORT

*t*hese support programs provide hope and guidance to children and their families.

SUPPORT PROGRAM	THIS PROGRAM DEALS WITH:
The Yellow Bus	Anxiety of starting school, study skills, peer pressure
Kids Hope	Terminal illness and death
You Can't Fool Me	Safety skills and protection from becoming lost, abducted, or abused
Character Counts	Develop qualities such as kindness, trust, patience, purity, love, gentleness, joy, self-control, truthfulness, peace, forgiveness
Homework Heaven	Homework assistance
United We Stand	Friendship and peer influence
Divorce Recovery for Kids	Parental separation and divorce
Viewpoint	Conflict resolution and problem solving

• **Service Programs**—These programs involve children in service opportunities and help children develop hearts for serving others. Service programs help children develop a servant attitude and a desire to make a positive difference in the world.

Service opportunities can be inside your children's ministry program or serve those who live in the larger community. You'll have to decide if you want one-shot, short-term projects or longer-term projects. Either way, keep service programs open to newcomers at all times. Service projects are great opportunities for children to develop friendships.

SERVICE

*t*hese service programs help children develop hearts for serving others.

SERVICE PROGRAM	DESCRIPTION
Kids' Servant Team	Service projects at the church and in the community
Puppet, Drama, Clown Ministry Teams	Write, create, act, perform
Multimedia Team	Operate sound board, lights, computers, video camera
Web Ministry	Design/update the children's Web site
Band and Praise Choir	Practice and perform
Kids' Welcome and Hospitality Team	Meet and greet kids who attend, make cards, write notes, call classmates

• **Discipleship**—These programs build a community of kids who want to grow deep in their Christian faith. These programs aren't for first-time visitors or sporadic attendees. They're designed to help children dive deeper into spiritual development as they study the Word of God, pray, develop friendships with other believers, and share testimonies. Children experience a personal relationship with Jesus and also disciple others as they build up each other's faith.

Discipleship classes can be long- or short-term but are intentionally more intimate so that children connect with each other. Experiences in which children encounter God and make life-changing decisions are the bull's-eye of the target. That's where you want every child to ultimately end up.

DISCIPLESHIP

these discipleship programs encourage children to deepen in their faith.

DISCIPLESHIP PROGRAM	DESCRIPTION
Young Believers	Explore Christianity and sacraments
The Bible Adventure	Study and apply the Word of God to everyday life situations
Prayer 101	Importance of a prayer life
Stewardship	Obedient giving and tithing
Readers' Choice	Read Christian books and discuss
Special Needs Class	Special classes for special kids who aren't mainstreamed
Special Interest Groups	Study and explore interests in different subjects
Mission Trip	Travel and perform a service project in another community

Starting a New Program

Something you'll discover early in your ministry is that church members are *great* at thinking up new ideas. They schedule meetings, share their dreams, provide information, and then leave your office expecting the dreams to become reality with the wave of a magic wand. Getting caught in the trap of always trying to make the dreams happen can take all the fun out of your ministry.

Answering the following questions *before* you begin any new program will let you determine up front whether the program will be meaningful to your children and church. Plus, investing time in planning before you launch the program will help you equip leaders for success during implementation.

• **Who will lead?** Aim always to have ministry be *lay-leader* driven. You shouldn't be the one teaching the class, planning the event, or doing the ministry. Rather, your job is to equip lay-leaders to do ministry and then provide a connection between the ministry leaders and the church.

In his book *Doing Church as a Team*, Wayne Cordeiro suggests that before launching a new program, our first step needs to be building a team of four leaders with whom the program leader can serve. This program ministry team becomes a support system that shares responsibilities and ownership of the program and provides a place for leaders to be accountable to each other. A strong team also helps prevent frustration and burnout.

It's important to accurately predict the number of servants needed to support a program, too. Do you have enough leaders? the right leaders? Are they equipped? all on the same page regarding the vision?

• **What will you do?** Here's where the time you spent researching your community pays off. To be meaningful, any program you develop must connect people with an experience they'll value or fill a need or interest. Meaningful programs also build a bridge to your church and a relationship with your church family.

Have you taken into consideration the culture and daily life of kids you want to reach? found a name for the program that creates interest and is inviting? decided precisely what need you'll meet?

• **When will you meet?** Timing is important. Schedule a day of the week and a time in the day when it's convenient for families to attend. Be considerate of and sensitive to young children and their routines.

Make sure you've also considered *God's* timing for the program. Great program ideas move forward and become a reality only with God's blessing. You may be able to recognize God's timing for your program as you evaluate how easily the components of your action plan come together. What would happen if you chose to not launch a program until you had all the volunteers you need in place?

• **Where will you meet?** Whether you have a huge facility or a tiny one, space is always an issue. Be creative as you search for the ideal location.

Some events and classes need to be held at your church building, but others may be appropriate for a neighborhood park, community building, or back yard. Growing a children's ministry may require you to go where the kids are.

Don't fail to take into consideration what supplies you'll need and what setup is required when thinking about where you should meet!

• **Why are you considering doing this new program?** Is it aligned with your church's overall goals and children's ministry philosophy? What's your desired outcome? Will you expand your current children's ministry, offer support to children and their families, provide service to your community, or develop disciples? In what ways will it engage kids and move them toward the center of the target?

• **How will you move ahead?** This question may be the most important to answer completely. Why? Because your answer becomes your action plan for making the proposed program a reality. You'll sort out the goals of the program, as well as a projected budget. This is the time to decide what publicity and promotion you'll need, who'll pay for what, and how your team will communicate. And decide right up front how you'll evaluate your effectiveness so that you can make midcourse corrections.

But it isn't *just* a matter of logistics. A detailed plan also helps make sure that your program will be meaningful for children and volunteers. Remember that what counts most isn't pulling off a spectacular event. What counts most is what's learned and how relationships develop during the course of the event—from the initial brainstorming meeting to sweeping up after the event ends.

Hit the Target!

Anyone can pull together a slapdash program to entertain kids. But to create a *meaningful* program requires something more.

It requires that you be intentional about selecting or building a program that's relevant to your kids, that meets the needs of your church and community, that's radical in it's creativity and uniqueness.

Meaningful programs also reflect God's love and mirror how kids learn and what kids already love to do. And nothing is more important than crafting programs that encourage transforming relationships.

Creating excellent children's programming is hard work, but it's rewarding, too. You'll touch kids' lives in ways that have a life-long impact and draw children closer to God.

It's worth the effort!

What Is Your Program Plan?

WHO is your...

staff contact?

leadership team (at least five individuals)?
1.
2.
3.
4.
5.

WHAT is your...

primary purpose?

program idea?

program description?

program theme?

program name?

estimated number of servants needed to support the program?

estimated attendance?

desired ministry outcome?

need for child care?

WHEN will you...

meet? What day of the week?

start? What time will your program begin?

end? What time will you wrap up?

do setup and tear-down? →

OK TO COPY

WHERE will...

you host the event?

you get supplies? And what supplies do you need?

you get the special equipment you need?

What equipment do you need?

WHY do you see this program as...
connected to your church mission?

consistent with your children's ministry philosophy?

relevant?

radical?

reflective?

relational?

HOW will your program look?
Specific activities or experiences:

Budget and financial support information:

Publicity and promotion efforts:

Communication timelines:

Evaluation:

seventeen

Sunday School From Start to Finish

by Barbara Younger and Lisa Flinn

For many churches, Sunday school is the heart of children's ministry. Even for churches that offer a wide range of children's programs, Sunday school may be your primary corporate teaching opportunity.

So it's vital to develop effective and creative approaches that will maximize your impact and make the Christian education you provide memorable and life-changing for children in your care. This chapter covers the basics of teaching Sunday school—from choosing curriculum to evaluating a lesson when it's finished.

Setting Up Classrooms

Your challenge is to make classrooms child-friendly and flexible. In each class space, hang a bulletin board for messages, art, and photographs. Mount bulletin boards and white boards at your children's eye level so that children can use them too. Have a cabinet, shelf, or rolling caddy to hold supplies, books, a tape or CD player, and games. Use furniture that can easily be moved to accommodate active group games, or consider using no furniture at all.

If you have little space and many children, be creative with meeting areas. Consider how to make use of a quiet hallway, an empty choir room, or the church lawn during warm weather.

For each age group, consider these classroom setups:

• **Babies**—Safety and comfort are the most important concerns with this age group. Examine cribs, seats, walkers, changing tables, and toys for loose, missing, or broken parts. Label cubbies, bins, or hooks that hold each baby's diaper bag and outerwear. Have comfortable rockers and other chairs for nursery workers. See Chapter 12 for more in-depth information on nurseries.

• **Toddlers**—Toddlers delight in small tables, chairs, and play kitchens. Set up the room for play, with enough toys to prevent confrontations between children.

• **Preschoolers**—Set up learning centers and play areas for three- to five-year-olds. For example, you might want to have a housekeeping corner, an area for children to dress up in different clothes, and an area with toy cars and trucks. Also have a table with nature items, a table with blocks, and another table for Play-Doh.

• **Elementary-age children**—For children in grades 1–6, leave an open area for activities such as games and drama. Have a Bible resource center equipped with Bible activities and books. Set up centers for projects that children can work on from week to week. Consider creating a pen pal center, a Bible characters costume corner, and an art center.

Choosing Curriculum and Resources

The key resource in your classrooms is curriculum. So before you choose one, review material from several publishers. Walk through two or three lessons as if you're actually teaching a group of children, noting what teaching methods are used and how activities will work in your classrooms. Check with your church leadership so that you're absolutely clear about your Christian education program's priorities and goals. Select curriculum that meets those goals and reflects your values about ministry with children. If you haven't yet articulated your vision and priorities, start there. See Chapter 1 for more information about that process.

The "Curriculum Evaluation Checklist" (pp. 190-191) will help you sort out what curriculum will best meet your needs.

The Supply Closet

In addition to getting curriculum, you'll need to stock your classroom supply closet. One easy way to collect nonperishable, "standard" craft supplies is to place a list where members of your church can see it. Ask adults to select one item, take it off the list, and donate the materials.

Gather basics such as right- and left-handed scissors, pencils, markers, crayons, glue, tape, staplers, a hole punch, and construction and writing paper. You may want to group items in topical kits. For example, a Noah's ark kit might include a picture book, a toy ark, a pattern for paper doves, and rainbow stickers.

Encourage all teachers to read through their lesson plans at least three days before the day they're scheduled to teach so that they'll know if specific supplies such as glitter or straws are needed. Some leaders read through the entire year's curriculum (or at least a quarter's) and order supplies all at once.

Curriculum Evaluation Checklist

Use or adapt the following worksheet for choosing your Sunday school curriculum.

OVERALL EVALUATION	YES	NO
Are objectives clearly stated, measurable, and attainable?	❑	❑
Are lessons based on biblical truths?	❑	❑
Are the theology and perspective compatible with your church or denomination?	❑	❑
Is the lesson presented in a manner that will engage your children?	❑	❑
Are lessons relational—helping children develop deeper relationships with God, each other, and the teacher?	❑	❑
Are lessons experiential—actively involving children in the lessons?	❑	❑
Are lessons applicable to children's daily lives?	❑	❑
Are a variety of learning styles engaged and used to communicate a lesson's Bible truth?	❑	❑
Do activities and experiences affirm students and make them feel good about themselves?	❑	❑
Are the activities fun for children?	❑	❑
Are the activities and methods creative?	❑	❑
Does the curriculum include appropriate worship and devotion ideas?	❑	❑
Are songs suggested? Do the suggestions reflect a variety of styles and tempos?	❑	❑
Are craft ideas age-appropriate?	❑	❑

OK TO COPY

→

OVERALL EVALUATION, cont.	YES	NO
Are materials included or readily available?	☐	☐
Are games related to the Bible story or Bible point?	☐	☐
Are games noncompetitive?	☐	☐
Does the curriculum provide both small- and large-group activities?	☐	☐
Are visuals large, bright, and sturdy?	☐	☐
Is the art age-appropriate and engaging?	☐	☐

TEACHER GUIDE	YES	NO
Is the guide easy to use?	☐	☐
Is the amount of preparation required appropriate for your volunteers' schedules?	☐	☐
Are tips provided to help teachers deal with special needs or problems?	☐	☐
Are options provided within lessons to give teachers choices?	☐	☐
Are lessons easily adaptable to your specific situation?	☐	☐

STUDENT MATERIALS	YES	NO
Are materials colorful and age-appropriate?	☐	☐
Are the student materials actually useful? Do they include a take-home element?	☐	☐
Are students challenged to make appropriate personal application of Bible truth?	☐	☐

Add to Your Curriculum

The word *curriculum* customarily refers to the print materials used for teaching, along with the accompanying media and student materials. But in a broader sense, *curriculum*, which comes from Latin and means "the course of one's life," might also include worship, service projects, fellowship, and Bible study. So it's completely appropriate to add to your teaching activities such as these:

• Organize a monthly potluck supper for a Sunday school class. Have the toddlers' families take turns hosting the group. Hire a teenage baby sitter to entertain the toddlers after the meal while the parents discuss jobs, marriage, toys, and parenting styles. Consider doing this for each classroom occasionally.

• Invite guests to your classrooms to share their faith stories and experiences. A dentist who volunteered at a clinic in Haiti can speak about what it means to be merciful. A teenager who served at a Group Workcamp[1] last summer can share about serving others. Survey your congregation to find people willing to share their stories.

• Field trips into God's world are insightful at any age. The fretful toddler who cries when dropped off at Sunday school may forget her fears while taking a walk to collect pretty leaves. Fifth-graders will experience learning Psalm 23 differently if they're standing in a field, pretending to herd sheep.

• When attendance fluctuates during the holidays and summer, consider combining classes into one large, multi-aged class. For example, hold an Epiphany party. Have children read the story from Matthew, play a follow-the-star game, eat star-shaped cookies, and sing "We Three Kings of Orient Are."

Age-Appropriate Teaching Activities

*t*eaching works best when you choose activities that fit the children's developmental stage. This chart gives an overview.

AGE	ACTIVITIES
12 to 18 months	**Art:** finger paints, large crayons **Drama:** puppets, dress-up hats, animal-sound games **Music:** noisemakers, singing, clapping **Games:** Peekaboo, Patty-cake **Play:** shape sorters, soft-shape toys, rolling toys **Ratios:** two infants to one adult, four toddlers to one adult **Attention Span:** can vary by second and by minute*
18 months to 3 years	**Art:** nontoxic paints, paper-plate masks, Play-Doh **Drama:** finger puppets, dress-up, imitating animals **Music:** clapping, rhythm instruments, group singing, recordings **Games:** circle games, leader games, Mother Goose games **Play:** housekeeping, push-pull toys, blocks, dolls **Ratios:** five children to one adult **Attention Span:** 1½ to three minutes*
3 to 5 years	**Art:** clay modeling, cutting, paper-bag puppets, collage **Drama:** masks and puppets, finger plays, flannel boards **Music:** songs with motions, recordings, rhythm instruments **Games:** movement games, circle games, guessing games **Play:** play sets, housekeeping, blocks, puzzles, dolls **Ratio:** eight children to one adult **Attention Span:** three to five minutes* →

AGE	ACTIVITIES
5 to 9 years	**Art:** papier-mâché, murals, clay projects **Drama:** skits, role-plays **Music:** songs with motions, foreign language songs, instruments, choir **Games:** games that switch directions and rules, board games **Play:** housekeeping, play sets, craft sets, block sets **Ratio:** twelve children to one adult in large groups, five children to one adult in small groups **Attention Span:** five to nine minutes*
9 to 12 years	**Art:** various paint mediums, clay sculpture, fabric banners **Drama:** plays, readings, clowning, pantomime **Music:** reading notes, instruments, singing in rounds **Games:** team games with more steps, individual skill games **Play:** collections, models, sports, challenging puzzles **Ratio:** maximum of fifteen children to one adult in large groups, seven children to one adult in small groups **Attention Span:** nine to twelve minutes per task*

*Children may stick with an activity much longer, but a good rule of thumb is one minute for each year; for example, two minutes for a two-year-old, eight minutes for an eight-year-old.

Preparing a Lesson

Train your teachers to always read ahead in their curriculum at least a month before teaching a lesson. Too many teachers teach from week to week without understanding the scope of their curriculum. Later these teachers realize they could have tied lessons together with an ongoing craft project or a special room decor.

Most lesson plans are based on Scripture. Have teachers read relevant passages carefully. Teachers must determine how the Scripture relates to the lesson objectives and ask themselves *why* children should learn about their lesson topic. If teachers don't understand the related Scripture or can't quickly explain why the lesson content is applicable to children's lives, children won't have much reason to listen or care.

After teachers become familiar with their Bible lessons, encourage them to be creative in deciding how to present them. Some curriculums include creative options, such as crafts, music, drama, games, and discussions. Part 2 of this book provides in-depth information about encouraging active, engaging, life-impacting learning.

Train your teachers to incorporate these tips in their lesson preparation:

• If teachers intend to read a story directly from the Bible, they must know it so well that they can read with expression. Eye contact keeps children engaged, and it's extremely important that teachers can pronounce Bible names and places with ease. And while reading aloud can be tremendously effective, it's important to use this technique in moderation.

• Teachers need to keep an eye on the clock while preparing a lesson. How long it takes to do an activity will vary widely depending on which students are in class, whether a discussion takes off, and whether the activity "clicks" with students. As teachers prepare, have them jot notes in their teacher books with an approximate time the activity should begin or end. But even with excellent planning, having an extra game or discussion launcher up a teacher's sleeve can be a lifesaver. Suggest that deciding on such "time stuffers" be part of preparation.

• Finally, ask teachers to pray before preparing any lesson. Remind teachers that God is with them as they prepare lessons.

Ask teachers to keep photos of their classroom regulars on their refrigerators and pray for their students as they reach for the milk. One teacher prays this prayer as she sits down to prepare a lesson: "Dear God, let the words of my mouth and the meditation of my heart be acceptable in your sight. Amen."

Teaching the Lesson—Tips for Your Teachers

Teaching starts before any children show up. Have teachers arrive in their classrooms at least fifteen minutes before their class begins. That time is the difference between being prepared (Are the materials you need ready? Do you have enough chairs? Did the youth group use the room last night and leave pizza boxes on the floor? Has the CD player disappeared? Are your storytelling props, craft supplies, and snacks tucked away out of sight until you need them?) and having to frantically scramble. Teachers who arrive in time to handle the details before children arrive will be calm and composed when it's time to teach.

Children usually don't arrive all at once. Encourage your teachers to engage the early birds in relationship-building discussion about how the past week went. One simple technique is to draw a line on the white board with a "1" at one end, and a "10" on the other. Children rank their weeks from "1" (the worst week of the child's life) to "10" (the best week ever). Children place their initials on the line anywhere but on "5" (because no one has a truly average week) and then explain why the week was ranked as it was. This gives your teachers insight into their children's lives and helps teachers make lessons applicable. And if six out of ten children report that they were up most of the night at a friend's birthday sleepover, that's important information to have *before* starting a lesson that includes a lengthy time of silent prayer!

The best teachers greet their students warmly. If teachers are new, have children wear name tags to help teachers learn names quickly. And the teacher should wear a name tag too!

Plan for distractions. In each classroom designate a specified "treasure box" or shelf on which to place any distracting objects children bring from home. Children need to know their treasures will be safe and cared for before they'll surrender the objects and engage in the lesson.

Also, agree on a nonverbal signal for teachers to use. It's how teachers will tell children it's time to begin class or focus on the teachers. Some teachers flash the lights. Others blow on a soft whistle or ring a bell. Whatever teachers choose to do, make sure that the sound isn't overly harsh and that it's accompanied with a gentle verbal reminder: "We have lots of fun things to do today, so let's move on so we can get to all of them."

Successful classes often begin with a creative, fun game or other activity that ties to the lesson. An activity will build interest, help kids focus, and help children feel comfortable with each other and their teacher.

When moving from activity to activity, have teachers allow a few minutes of transition time and give clear directions. And let teachers know they needn't feel discouraged if some children don't participate in every activity. Adam may refuse to sing, or Maria may balk at putting her hands in finger paints. Observing which students respond to which activities will let teachers discover students' learning styles and be better able to tailor future lessons to reach each learner.

Giving kids choices avoids most discipline problems. Offer Shawn the option of writing a poem about Jonah and the large fish or painting a picture of them instead. Either way, Shawn interacts with the lesson. And if he still refuses to participate, there's no reason to insist. Shawn may not feel secure in trying something new. Have teachers encourage children for their efforts, never for the results.

Know what to do if things fall flat. If a project bombs completely, for whatever reason, have teachers quickly move on to something else. But if the class is really enjoying an activity, there's no need to rush it. Have teachers trim something else from the lesson.

Children *love* snacks. Young children may expect a snack every week. Older children don't need a snack each time, but they'll certainly enjoy having one. Coordinate snacks to Bible stories and verses so snack time can be a teaching time, too. For example, animal crackers are perfect when learning about Noah's ark.

Ending a Class

Encourage your teachers to wrap up lessons in a positive, memorable way by incorporating these techniques in their teaching:

• Review at the end of class what you wanted to teach. Review reinforces the lesson and helps you determine if the children understood the material. Ask children what they liked best and least about the lesson. Don't let their responses hurt your feelings; rather, use their feedback as an evaluation tool.

• Some teachers end class each week with the same activity, such as a circle prayer or special song. One teacher lights a candle and asks everyone to gather for a silent prayer. Another teacher has the children add an item such as a sticker, fabric shape, or magazine picture to a wall collage. Each item reflects, in some way, the week's lesson.

Occasionally send home a small present such as a pencil, button, or magnet imprinted with a Christian message. Homemade modeling dough, a ribbon Bible bookmark, or a Band-Aid (use this when you teach about the good Samaritan!) are other ideas. However you choose to end your class, say a personal goodbye to each child, making eye contact with each child. Thank each child for coming to your class.

Handling Behavior Problems

Below are some common behavior problems you may encounter in
teaching children of different ages.

AGE	PROBLEM	WAYS TO RESPOND
Birth to 18 months	Fussing, crying Feeling hurt or frightened Fighting	• Meet basic needs such as feeding or changing. • Remove source of irritation. • Comfort with singing or rocking. • Assure with a hug, smile, or kind words. • Remove the object, such as a scary jack-in-the-box. • Redirect attention to new toys. • Help kids share by dividing toys.
19 months to 3 years	Saying "no" Fighting, not sharing	• Set simple rules. • Be firm and even-tempered. • Give choices. • Redirect attention to a new toy or activity. • Take away objects in dispute or suggest ways to cooperate. • Comfort with a hug or kind words.
4 to 5 years	Fighting, not sharing	• Help with taking turns. • Suggest a different activity. • Separate children.
6 to 12 years	Disrupting lesson Reluctant attitudes	• Repeat class rules. • Appoint helpers. • Affirm positive behavior. • Make lessons more active. • Remove child, if necessary. • Provide fun and interesting activities. • Acknowledge children's preferences. • Have midweek contacts and group get-togethers.

Evaluating Your Teaching

Once the class ends, teaching isn't over. Teachers need to form the habit of reviewing the lesson at home. What went well? What didn't? What would they do differently next time? Thoughtful, candid reflection will help teachers make subsequent lessons stronger.

And Christian education directors or Sunday school superintendents can provide valuable feedback by observing classes quarterly or every six months and sharing their observations. Volunteer teachers *want* to know how they're doing and to improve in their teaching.

Ask teachers to pray for students who were absent and to write or call them. Some teachers have found that a midweek contact helps ensure more consistent attendance. And timely contacts communicate love and concern.

A caring teacher who communicates truth clearly and kindly is a tremendous asset in the lives of children. It's absolutely true that a Sunday school class can become an anchor in a child's otherwise unpredictable life. Your Sunday school classrooms are more than places to transmit information. They can also be places where young lives are transformed.

Endnote

1. Group Workcamps are the premier one-week youth group summer service projects. For more information call 1-800-447-1070.

eighteen
Children and Congregational Worship

by Ben F. Freudenburg

As a leader in your church's children's ministry, you have an important opportunity. You can shape how children in your church value worship and, through how your church worships, help your congregation value your children.

Many churches separate children and adults when it's time to worship. God can certainly use child-only worship experiences, but I'd like you to consider *not* segregating children during congregational worship times. Rather, deliberately integrate children *into* the corporate worship experience.

What I'm asking is that you create *family-friendly* congregational worship experiences. And that means including children.

I've visited churches where there are no children present in congregational worship and wondered what impact that will have on the worship life of the next generation. I've been in congregational worship and watched children be led out of the service just before the pastor started to preach. I wondered what that model taught those children about listening to God's spoken Word.

And I've been in churches that *included* children in congregational worship and noticed a different level of excitement and significance in those gathered for worship. I had to wonder what impact that had on the life of the church and the faith life of those children.

Where *do* children belong during congregational worship? For a children's ministry leader, this isn't just a logistics question; it's a *worship* question.

Take this quick quiz to discover what you believe. Do you agree or disagree with these statements?

___ Children belong in the main worship gathering of your congregation.

___ Children grow in knowledge and faith through congregational worship.

___ Deliberate involvement of children in worship should be done in all congregational worship settings.

___ The most important years of faith development are age two years through second grade, and worship is a main event in a child's faith development.

___ Corporate congregational worship should be prepared through the eyes of children.

___ Parents are the primary worship mentors and teachers in your congregation.

Well? Where do you stand? These questions get at your current beliefs about whether children belong in congregational worship settings alongside adults, whether children actually *can* worship, and what your role should—or shouldn't—be in facilitating children's worship in a congregational worship setting.

Let me share some thoughts about the importance of including children in congregational worship.

Children belong in congregational worship because...

• worship is one place where age holds no power. Children can be accepted as fully able to worship God and sense they're important and valued by God and his people.

• a child's relationship with God and the Christian community is developed through child-friendly congregational worship. That's hard to do without including children in congregational worship.

• worship is a family time. It's a time to *connect* families rather than separate them. It's a time when children can hear and see the faith of their parents. Congregational worship is a place where children can have uninterrupted time with Mom and Dad. It's a shared experience that, if done appropriately, can build deep faith memories.

• congregational worship is a time for parents to pass on the faith to the next generation with the help of the church. Congregational worship is a place where parents, grandparents, brothers, and sisters can experience the things of faith as creeds are spoken, sins are confessed and forgiven, prayers are lifted, songs and hymns of the church are sung, Scripture is read, and the traditions of the church are observed and celebrated.

• children form strong opinions about congregational worship based on their experiences. These opinions about worship and its value are carried into the children's adult lives, so we're wise to plan congregational worship to include children in a meaningful, positive way.

Convinced? Good. Let that conviction prompt you to work your way through the process described below.

STEP ONE:
Make an Appointment With Your Pastor

Ask to meet with your pastor to discuss involving children in congregational worship. Invite the music leader and anyone else responsible for the worship service to the meeting.

Your agenda is to discover where they stand on the issue. Remember that you're not responsible for developing the worship service; you're responsible for the children you serve. It's your job to make sure that children are included in the worship life of your church, but all your suggestions as to precisely how to accomplish that may not be adopted.

When you meet with your pastor and other worship leaders, ask them to take the quick quiz presented earlier in this chapter. Listen to their answers. Read some of the bulleted points in this chapter aloud, and ask your leaders to respond. Discover what they believe. If you find they're open to congregational worship that includes kids, you may want to share this chapter with them and set a follow-up appointment to discuss ways to proceed.

STEP TWO:
Develop a Class That Trains Parents
to Worship With Children

Your most important worship resource is parents. The pastor, children's minister, and music director influence how worship impacts kids, but parents make the biggest impact regarding how children experience and view worship. That's why it's important to provide training for parents about worshipping with their kids.

Your parent training should include:

• Teaching parents the importance of congregational worship for their children.

• Helping parents learn the proper manners for children at worship. Don't forget talking about making a trip to the bathroom before worship services start and the need for parents to arrive five minutes early so they can help children get ready for worship.

• Helping parents teach children the songs and hymns you'll use and how to use the worship resources you provide.

• Training parents to be worship educators and tutors. Be sure parents know how to worship God. They can't train their children in things they don't understand themselves.

• Teaching parents how to discipline children in a congregational worship setting. You may choose to instruct them to remove their children from the service for a discussion outside or recommend another approach. Be clear and specific.

• Helping parents understand the "rules and regulations" for congregational worship at your church. Many rules are unwritten and unspoken, and the only way one knows a rule has been broken is by the stares one gets from other members. Being on the receiving end of raised eyebrows or condemning stares often terrifies parents.

Think you don't have any rules? Then turn to a neighbor during the sermon next week and speak loudly enough to be heard six feet away. Interrupt the sermon by raising your hand and asking a question. Ask an usher if you can change seats. Make change for a twenty from the offering plate when it passes by. Ask for seconds during communion. You'll find out that you have rules!

Parents who tutor or mentor their children during congregational worship may discover a new bond developing with their children. They may also find their children can't *wait* for worship, because the children receive the attention they crave from Mom or Dad.

You don't have to create or teach this class on your own. Rather, develop a partnership and have the pastor, the music leader, preschool teachers, and other members of the staff or leaders in the church help you develop and lead it.

STEP THREE:
Create Congregational Worship With Children in Mind

It's best to not make big changes all at once. Rather, start with one small step. Let's call it child-friendly tweaking. Consider the following:

Announcements—One simple way to start is to have announcements that are directed at the children. Why *not* announce programs that affect children in a congregational setting?

Hymns and songs—Add a children's song that fits the theme of the worship. If you have a children's message, have the congregation sing a children's song as the children come forward. It could be the same song each Sunday. Many great hymns have simple refrains you could teach children in Sunday school so that the songs could be sung during congregational worship. Have a hymn of the month. Record the hymn on tape with children's voices, and give the tape to parents to play in the car or at home. Teach the hymn in the congregational worship after preparing children to help teach it.

Scripture readings—Think of ways for children to connect with Scripture readings. Give a word of the day, and have them repeat that word every time it is spoken. Prepare children to be the Scripture readers. It's amazing how children pay attention when one of their own reads. There are many creative ways to honor children through the reading of the Scripture in worship!

Prayers—Have children submit prayer requests to the pastor, and include those requests in the prayers on Sunday. Teach a simple congregational response to be used during the prayers of the day so that children can also join in. A simple response is "Lord, hear our prayers." Each week, include in the prayers thanks for each child having a birthday in the coming week. Pray for these children by name.

Sermon—Keep the sermon to twenty minutes, but use seven minutes for the children's message and thirteen minutes for the adult sermon. If the pastor preaches both sermons, use the children's message to introduce the theme of the sermon. If another person does the children's message, have the pastor and that person work together, finding ways to make the two into one.

If you're the person responsible for the children's message, here are "12 Children's Message Do's." These twelve "do's" come from the book *Through Children's Eyes: 52 Worship Talks for Children*.[1] They assume the children's message fits into the adult sermon theme.

1. Do write it out.
2. Do memorize it.
3. Do practice it.
4. Do anticipate the movement and response of the children.
5. Do have only one point or truth to your message.
6. Do involve the children, but don't let them get out of control.
7. Do experiment, have fun, and celebrate.
8. Do keep the message and its language age-appropriate.
9. Do bring children into the presence of God and let them sense his wonder.
10. Do include directions for the congregation.
11. Do have handouts to reinforce the message.
12. And most important: Do include the gospel in every message.

STEP FOUR:
Create Child-Friendly Worship Spaces and Resources

Can children see the action during congregational worship? If not, add booster chairs so they can. Or how about saving the front seats for families with small children? Do you have a space for parents to take kids who are acting up? Is there a place to take children out of the worship services that provides the privacy one needs for breast-feeding without having to miss the service?

Inviting families with children to worship with the rest of the congregation doesn't mean abolishing the nursery. Having an excellent nursery communicates that, while children are welcome in worship, a nursery is an option if a parent needs it. For a great checklist to consult when setting up or reviewing a church nursery, see pages 142-143.

And consider offering children's worship resources to help kids get the most out of worship. Some options include children's bulletins, activity bags, worship clipboards, and offering envelopes for kids. You might even create a kids' worship center just outside the corporate worship space where kids can pick up their worship resources.

STEP FIVE:
Involve Kids in Worship by Using Their Gifts and Talents

You know you belong when your community cherishes your gifts and abilities and wants you to use them. It's important that we let children experience that reassuring emotion.

Most churches love children's choirs and bell choirs, but how about a kids' wind ensemble, brass choir, or guitar choir? Can a young artist design a bulletin cover or a budding dancer share a dance of praise? Can a child read the Scripture? Can children serve as worship helpers? The answer is a resounding *yes*!

When you cherish children's gifts, they'll know they really belong and are valued by the community of faith and the God that community serves.

STEP SIX:
Provide Thorough Worship Team Training

Pastors, ushers, greeters, altar guild members, and all others who are part of your Worship Team need to be trained to cherish and honor children in worship.

Training needs to include practical things: age-appropriate language skills, making eye contact, the art of greeting children (hint: It helps if you can kneel!), and seeing worship through children's eyes. These simple habits can add much to children's worship experiences.

Children are important to the Christian community. They're precious and important to God. When Jesus said, "Let the little children come to me, and do not hinder them," he was sending a very clear signal that worship includes kids. They can and should come into the presence of God. Congregational worship *must* include kids.

Consider the message any other model sends to children. They're excluded, either by default or intent. Does that communicate that we're too busy for children? that they aren't important enough? that the love of God is only for grown-ups? that the teachings of Scripture are too complex for children to grasp?

And what message is sent to homes with children? That we know what's best for your children, and it's being separated from you as you worship?

I believe the church needs children in worship for the sake of the children, their homes, and the church. Children's presence in congregational worship builds their knowledge and faith in God and impacts how they value and view worship later in life. It only makes sense for us to plan worship to include all ages—*especially* children.

ENDNOTE

1. Ben F. Freudenburg, *Through Children's Eyes: 52 Worship Talks for Children* (St. Louis, MO: Concordia Publishing House, 1996).

nineteen

Children's Church: Leading Children Into Worship

by Beth Rowland

People were created to worship.

In culture after culture, throughout history, people have worshipped. Worship is such an innate need that people, given no other option, will go so far as to worship rocks and sticks. Worship is a big deal! We all worship something.

As Christians we worship the one, true God revealed to us through Scripture. As a children's worker, you have the privilege of leading children to worship the one, true God. I can think of no greater opportunity than to lead kids in worship.

Which means children's church is a wonderful thing!

Lots of churches "do" children's church. But I think very few make the most of the opportunity because they

211

don't really understand what children's church can be.

Some churches tack on a singing time to the beginning of their Sunday school hour and call it worship. Some churches herd children together, show them an elaborate puppet play or drama, and call it worship. Some churches put all their kids in one room, sing a few songs, do an object lesson, and call it worship, because it requires fewer volunteers and they want to give their teachers a break.

None of these things are wrong. Kids love to sing. Kids love puppets, and sometimes volunteers *do* need a break. But we need a better understanding of what worship with kids can and should be. Worshipping the Creator of the universe is too important for us to approach it without considerable thought.

Chapter 1 of this book addresses the need to create a vision statement for your ministry. And assuming you've gone through the process, I think there's a good chance your statement includes your desire to have children know God—to have a deep personal relationship with their Lord and Savior. That's a great goal!

Now think about the programs you offer. Do they help children know God or know *about* God?

Many church programs for children stress kids learning Bible stories and Bible facts. Children learn about Abraham, David, Samuel, Paul, and other Bible personalities. They memorize Bible verses—John 3:16, Psalm 23, and other key Bible passages. They learn what God wants from them.

It's good to help children be biblically literate. But if we stop there, we haven't done enough for our kids.

If you want your kids to love God with all their heart, soul, and strength, then you have to provide children with time of real worship—time to reflect on who God is and what he has done and to simply be in awe of him.

Think about your own walk with God. How close would you feel to God if your total experience had been memorizing the names of all twelve disciples and charting Paul's missionary journeys? Those things are good to know, but they don't do much to draw us closer to our loving God.

Now think about a particularly precious moment of worship when your heart swelled to the point of bursting with gratitude to God and with wonder for how powerful and majestic he is. How close to God did you feel then? During which of those experiences did your love for God deepen?

When we worship God, we're filled with awe and wonder. We're moved to thank him, love him, and praise him. Our love for God and our commitment to God grows. It's through worship that God becomes real to us and we come to see him as our Abba Father.

Our kids deserve to have the opportunity to worship God.

Too often our children's programs seek to prepare kids to serve God at some point in the future. We approach Christian education the way we approach school, where a child has twelve to sixteen years to prepare to actively enter the work force.

But we aren't preparing children to get involved at some distant, indistinct future time. Our goal in Christian education is to help kids have a relationship with God *now*. That's not something you prepare for; it's something you do. And the more time kids spend with God talking to him, loving him, and worshipping him, the better their relationship with God will be.

Worship Comes in All Sizes

How do you start? How can you have a time of authentic worship with people who haven't fully mastered the multiplication tables and who are chewing gum while they're trying to sing?

It's important to realize that worship with kids looks different from worship with adults. Children think and act differently than adults, and their worship reflects those differences. But God accepts worship from both young and old, tall and small.

Here are some things to keep in mind as you prepare to lead children in worship:

Be culturally relevant. Kids are savvy consumers of culture, and like it or not, we have to meet children within their culture. Think of yourself as a missionary. If you were taking the gospel to a tribe in the remotest South American jungle that had never heard of Jesus, you would search for ways to make the gospel relevant to them. Kids have their own culture and their own way of understanding the world.

While we never want to compromise our message, it only stands to reason that we want to explain our message in terms of kids' culture. And video and computers speak louder to kids than flannel graphs and chalk talks these days.

Be age-appropriate. Have you ever sat behind a preschooler in an adult worship service? I've yet to meet a four-year-old who attentively listens to the sermon and can tell me what the pastor was trying to communicate. It's simply beyond a child's capabilities.

We shouldn't aim too high, but neither should we aim too low. Sixth-graders in your church probably listen to the same music that the youth listen to. If a child has just spent Saturday night at a live concert featuring the hottest Christian band on tour, you just can't ask him to sing "Jesus Wants Me for a Sunbeam" on Sunday morning. Not twice, anyway.

Here are some common elements of worship and tips on how to make sure you plan worship services that are relevant and appropriate for kids.

• **Music**—Music is *huge* because kids love music. There are plenty of theories about how to plan music for worship—what kinds of songs to sing and in what order you should sing them to draw people into worship. But it doesn't need to be that complicated.

You need to do two things: Choose music that kids love (if kids hate a song, they'll find it difficult to worship when singing it), and choose music that's worshipful. Worshipful music overtly talks about God and why he's worthy of worship. "I'm in the Lord's Army" might be a fun song, but it doesn't have much value as a worship song; it focuses entirely on the Christian and doesn't mention even one praiseworthy thing about God.

The rest is a combination of common sense and a sensitivity to your particular group of children. If you sing too many slow songs, kids get bored. If you sing too many fast songs, kids get hyper.

Consider your church, kids, and ministry goals when you plan music for your children's church. Some churches only sing hymns. Some churches only sing rock music. Some churches have kids who participate in a praise band. Other churches find it easier to sing along with CDs. All of these options are fine.

When you're planning the music for your children's church, include a repertoire of two or three dozen praise songs that your kids learn, and use them frequently. Each week, choose several songs from that basic list that tie into the worship theme of the day, occasionally teaching new songs so that your repertoire is always growing.

And don't be afraid to use some of the same music adults use in their worship service. A caution: Be careful to explain large words and tough theological concepts. Kids can understand a great deal, but only if things are clearly explained.

A music detail: Choose songs that are pitched for kids' voices. In general, don't go below the A below middle C, and don't go more than one octave above middle C.

• **Praise**—Praise is a vital element of worship, but it doesn't automatically happen just because children are singing.

Psalm 95 tells us to sing, but it also tells us to shout joyfully to the Rock of our salvation. Praise is telling God why he's good. That's what worship is all about.

Kids can worship through singing, shouts, and whispers. They can proclaim God's praise through artwork, games, music, and prayer. Praise is an excellent way to help kids process what they know about God. Children may have learned by hearing about Hannah that God answers prayer, but when they praise God by saying, "Lord, I praise you for answering Hannah's prayer and because you answer my prayers," they're *interacting* with God himself and recalling that God is available to them, too.

ere are some praiseworthy attributes of God to explore in your children's church:

God alone is God.	God is our rock.
God is creator.	God is our comfort.
God is faithful.	God is peace.
God is forgiving.	God is my helper.
God is love.	God is our shepherd.
God is strong.	God is our hope.
God defends us.	God is great and awesome.
God is our Father.	God is a father to the fatherless.

• **Prayer**—Prayer is connecting with God. And because one goal of our ministry to children is to help them develop strong relationships with God, kids need to pray.

But most children aren't wired to bow their heads and clasp their hands for extended periods. Nor do we want to teach kids that "assuming the position" is what prayer is all about. Prayer is communicating with God, and it needs to be as much a part of a child's life as breathing.

You can encourage children to pray by weaving all kinds of different prayers through your worship time. Have children pray prayers of thanksgiving and praise. Play prayer games. Have kids pray for each other in small groups. Have individuals pray for the entire group.

Prayer can be serious, and it can be fun, but kids who are put on the spot to pray in front of everyone often conclude that prayer is scary. Make prayer natural by including lots of opportunities for conversational prayer. Make prayer simple. Give kids specific things to pray for. Model prayer so children can see how it's done.

• **Bible Learning**—There's a world of difference between teaching the Bible in a Sunday school setting and in a children's worship setting.

Sunday school is our chance to teach kids the content they need to know: the characters, stories, themes, history, and significance—all that stuff. Worship needs to be set apart for something more sacred than education. Worship is a time to meet *with* God and to adore him for who he is and what he has done.

We still teach the Bible in a worship setting but with a different end in sight. In Sunday school, your goal might be for kids to know what happened to Abraham and why Abraham's faith in God is so important. But in children's church, you can help kids appreciate what God did for and through Abraham.

In Sunday school, you might want kids to learn the books of the Bible, the fruit of the Spirit, or the names of the twelve disciples. But in children's church your goal should never be to help kids absorb more Bible facts. Children's church is one of the rare times in children's lives when they're not preparing to do something that they won't be able to do until they're older. Children can worship *right now.* And they *need* to worship.

Children's encounter with Scripture during children's church should help them understand that God is awesome and does awesome things. No matter what Bible story or passage you base your worship session on, look to see what that Scripture reveals about God, and teach your kids to appreciate God's character and God's deeds as expressed in that passage.

• **Offering**—Giving back to God is a huge part of worship, but there are some practical considerations when planning an offering time for a group of people who don't have jobs.

You may have kids in your group who have more pocket money than you do! But as a general rule, offerings with kids need to be structured differently than for adults because you probably also have kids whose parents don't believe in allowances.

So here's what to do.

Always include an offering time in your children's worship time. It's a valuable lesson to learn that we can give of ourselves to God as an act of worship. But don't make *money* the main focus of your offering time. An offering is simply something that we offer to God because of our gratitude to him. Teach children that they can give of themselves. Children can give their talents, time, money, art, service, devotion, praise, and love to God.

One Sunday, you might have kids write songs to sing to God during an offering time. Another Sunday, you might have kids offer God a sacrifice of praise. Another Sunday, kids might draw an offering mural. Another Sunday, kids might bring in toys they no longer want, to give to others.

Another consideration: Young children have a hard time understanding the abstract concept of giving money to God. Make your offering as concrete as possible. When you do have offerings that center on money, use the money for a very specific purpose. For example, you might buy Bibles with the money and give them to children at a homeless shelter.

• **Ritual and Structure**—Think for a moment about your church's adult worship service. Whether your church is highly liturgical or simple in its approach to worship, it's likely that the adult worship service follows some kind of predictable format from week to week. That format helps people know what to expect and gives people a sense of comfort and tradition.

Kids need structure in their worship, too. As you create your children's church structure, keep in mind that kids find comfort in tradition. They like to know what's going to happen and when.

Create a format that helps kids feel anchored and secure. For example, you may always want to begin your children's church with a skit, or you may always begin your time with praise music.

Kids love a certain amount of ritual, too. Ritual can help children feel that their time of worship is special, sacred, and holy. Consider developing traditions for your children's church. Maybe it's keeping a special Bible in a special box and each week letting a different child open the box and bring out the Bible. Or you might start a tradition of praying by candlelight at the close of your worship service.

Keep in mind, however, that a little bit of ritual goes a *long* way. There's a difference between creating an atmosphere of holiness and just getting stuck in a rut.

• **Spectator Activities**—In most churches, children's church is the single largest gathering of kids. And with so many children in one room, it's hard to plan hands-on activities.

So it seems practical to have something happen in the front of the room that the kids can watch as a group. Maybe it's a video, skit, game show, or puppet show. With all of these, the kids are largely reduced to an audience, not participants.

Skits and videos can be great additions to your children's church program, but don't let them be the main event.

"Spectator activities" often don't help children actually worship God. And an entertaining video clip can quickly take kids' focus off God. Too often these big-group kinds of activities are actually just fun time fillers and do little to help move kids into worship and praise.

Also, in any big-group activity, it's hard to make sure that each child is engaged in what's happening. It's easy for children (and adults!) to tune out when they're just watching something happen. Do all you can to keep every child actively involved in everything that happens in children's church. Give children specific things to watch for in a video. Or ask children to call out a word or sound effect during a skit.

Balance spectator events with small-group activities. Look for creative ways to turn spectator events into small-group activities.

For instance, rather than having a large group prayer time where individuals call out prayer requests that the leader then prays about, have prayer time happen in small groups of three or four. Children can share what they want to pray about within their small groups and then pray in their groups.

Rather than ask children to raise their hands and call out possible answers to a question posed during a lesson, have kids do a "pair share." Each child turns to a partner and shares what he or she thinks the answer is, then the leader provides the answer. The result: Kids stay involved, and even shy children risk answering a question.

Art and service projects can be done quickly and effectively in small groups, too.

The point: Balance spectator activities with small-group activities. Every child should have a chance to praise, pray, and worship God in his or her heart. Every child *needs* to encounter God in your children's church!

I want to encourage you in your journey toward creating an awesome children's church time for the kids you serve. Creating a meaningful worship experience will do so much for your kids and their relationship with God. It is well worth your time to create an atmosphere in which children can praise their Savior. Let me tell you what happened in my church…

It was my first or second Sunday leading children's church with a small but "lively" group of third- and fourth-grade girls. And I was struggling.

The girls were doing their best to figure out how much they could get away with. They were good, sweet kids, but they were ornery with a creativity and a resourcefulness that I couldn't help but admire. And I really struggled to find a way to pull them into worshipping God.

But then we sang an absolutely gorgeous worship song that includes words from Psalm 107: "Give thanks to the Lord, for he is good; his love endures forever." After the song, I passed around a gift-wrapped box and asked each girl to hold it, to silently thank God for his goodness, and to write a word on the box that represented what she was thankful for.

Something amazing happened during that activity. I watched as each girl held the box and prayed. Right before my eyes, I saw those girls change. They stopped thinking about themselves, the class, and me. Instead, they started thinking about God.

One at a time, the girls silently thanked God, and a spirit of wonder and awe came over the room. And as each girl held the box and prayed prayers of thanksgiving, the countenance of each child brightened. They smiled gentle smiles.

It was a beautiful thing to see.

Those girls encountered a loving and mighty God that day. As they left the room, they were cheerful, quiet, and full of hugs for me.

I kept that box in the room for the rest of my time with those girls. And nearly every week one of them picked up the box and read the words they had written, asking if we could do the activity again.

I don't think those girls had ever had the opportunity to actually worship God before. Worshipping God changed them. It changed their attitudes, and it changed their understanding of God—and their relationship with him.

Creating a time of worship will change *your* kids, too! I'm sure of it!

twenty

Adventures in Vacation Bible School

by Jody Brolsma

Vacation Bible school is a great way to reach children and their families. Unfortunately, many churches are giving up on vacation Bible school. Everyone is busy; kids are involved in sports, music, and summer school; and volunteers seem non-existent. And these programs *can* be a lot of work. But with a little creativity and planning, vacation Bible school can become an exciting part of your children's ministry.

VBS: Why Bother?

Quite simply, because VBS has the potential to strengthen, energize, and expand your ministry in phenomenal ways.

Here are just a few of the fruits you can cultivate through a well-run, well-thought-out VBS program.

You'll reach kids in your community with the message of God's love. Most churches put on a VBS program because they want to reach outside the walls of the church to the kids in their communities. The VBS environment (complete with decorations, snacks, and music) is inviting to kids who otherwise might never set foot inside a church. This is a prime opportunity to get kids into your church and into God's Word!

You'll give the kids in your church the opportunity to grow closer to God. "Churched" kids who regularly attend Sunday school and children's ministry events benefit from a focused time of worship, Bible learning, and service. Use VBS as a time of discipleship to help kids grow in their faith. Plus, you can challenge kids to share their faith by bringing friends to VBS.

You'll get kids involved in missions. Many VBS curricula include a focus on missions, allowing children in your community to serve in practical ways. This is a great opportunity to open kids' eyes to new ways they can share God's love.

You'll grow your other children's ministries! Since VBS usually requires a number of volunteers, it's an excellent way to give people a "low-commitment" taste of children's ministry. And once they've had a blast at VBS, they're more likely to volunteer in other children's ministry programs.

You'll connect with families. VBS is a natural way to bring entire families into your church and to get to know families that already attend your church. Many churches have had great success with holding an evening "family VBS" in which families participate in all activities together.

A New Spin on an Old Idea

Not too long ago, VBS was less of an exciting children's ministry event and more of a weeklong summer Sunday school program. Be sure you've updated your thinking in order to meet the needs and expectations of today's kids—and adults. Think out of the box! Here are some things to consider:

• **What's your purpose?** Think through the purpose of your vacation Bible school. Ask, "Why are we having VBS?" Is it to attract kids from your community? Or is discipleship your focus? Some churches even use VBS as an opportunity for their youth group to serve and minister to children. Maybe you want to provide a time for families to spend together.

Now, as you consider how to use VBS in your church, keep your purpose in mind. It's easy to be distracted by all the "bells and whistles" like decorations, skits, and costumes for your volunteers. Be sure to spend your time and energy on things that connect *directly* to your vision.

• **When should we have VBS?** Why assume vacation Bible school must take place during one week of the summer during the day? Consider holding a one-day program or a weekend retreat for families. What about VBS for the entire family, and meeting in the evening? And why hold VBS only in the summer? What about other vacation times, such as Christmas break and spring break?

Many churches have discovered that evenings work best for them. More adults can help, the weather is cooler, and you can start with a simple meal for families to enjoy together.

• **What ages will you include?** Although most vacation Bible school curricula are designed for elementary-age kids, you may want to have a separate program for preschoolers, too. Some churches even have family vacation Bible schools where parents and teens have their own Bible classes and activities. However, remember that you have the unique opportunity to bring families *together* with VBS, so you may *not* want to design a program that will place them in separate classes.

• **Where will we have VBS?** Does VBS need to be held in your church? Absolutely not! Consider a local park or community center. Since many public schools are unused during the summer, check into holding your VBS there. Find the setting that will make your VBS the best!

Making VBS Easy

Regardless of the number of kids that will attend your vacation Bible school, this program is a *big* event. You'll need to coordinate everything from publicity to supplies and recruiting...and that's all *before* the actual week of VBS. Here are three ways to make your VBS easy and effective:

1. Avoid the temptation to write your own program. While writing your own curricula might save a few dollars, it will cost you enormously in the time, energy, and worry departments. There are countless VBS programs on the market, and one or more will be a good fit for your church. Take the time to choose a well-planned, field-tested program that offers support for you and your staff. You'll get Bible lessons, music, crafts, supply lists, publicity helps, decorating ideas, and more—without all the hassle and time of creating things from scratch.

2. Delegate, delegate, delegate! This should become your favorite word. Make VBS easy for each person involved by forming teams based on people's interests and gifts. Decorating teams can focus on transforming your church into a jungle or space station. A supply team will concentrate on rounding up everything from buckets to bungee cords. By delegating these responsibilities whenever possible, you not only free up your time for other things like training and recruiting, but you also allow volunteers to minister with their strengths.

3. Consider using a combined-age approach. Kids are with their peers in most children's ministry programs, so why not shake things up and use a multi-age approach for VBS? Although kids (and even parents) might protest at first, you'll discover that this is truly the easy way to go. You'll say goodbye to cliques and those "I'm-too-cool-for-church" preteen attitudes and say hello to cooperation, relationship-building, and teamwork. And discipline problems nearly disappear.

How to Select a VBS Curriculum

A trip to your local Christian bookstore will open your eyes to the VBS programs on the market. Their packaging and themes are dazzling, but which one is right for your church? Which one will be the most effective at helping kids know Jesus? Here are a few questions to consider as you look over VBS curricula.

• **What methods are used to teach the lesson?** Are kids involved in the story, or are they simply read to? Put yourself in a child's position. At the end of the lesson, what would you walk away with?

• **Do the student materials have lasting value?** Will students use the materials after VBS, or will the materials end up in the trash?

• **Will the music interest today's kids?** Can the songs be learned quickly? Does the music provide year-round or one-time use?

• **Will the crafts capture kids' imaginations?** Are they different, fun, high-quality? Do they reinforce the Bible theme or story?

• **At the end of the week, what will kids walk away with?** After two months, what will kids remember?

The Ultimate VBS Planning Guide

The first step in planning for VBS is setting the dates. (Be sure to check your church calendar to ensure that your dates don't conflict with other church functions.) Then use this planning guide to keep your VBS on track and chugging ahead.

SIX MONTHS BEFORE VBS

- Enlist a VBS director—maybe even two!
- Form committees for things like decorating, publicity, and supplies.
- Set a budget and determine what (if any) fund-raisers you can do.

THREE MONTHS BEFORE VBS

- Begin recruiting volunteers. (This will be an ongoing process!)
- Order your curriculum and supplies such as crafts and student materials.
- Plan and schedule a staff-training meeting.

TWO MONTHS BEFORE VBS

- Start publicity efforts. Create a buzz about your awesome program!
- Begin gathering supplies.
- Connect with your staff on any questions they might have.

ONE MONTH BEFORE VBS

- Begin preregistration. Remember, you'll have an easier time planning if you have an idea of how many kids will be there.
- Hold a staff-training meeting.
- Do a walk-through of your facility to plan where different events will take place.

Then enjoy your creative, life-changing vacation Bible school!

Ten Tips for Getting VBS Kids to Come to Sunday School

You've just finished a tremendous, high-energy, dynamic VBS program. Now what? How do you funnel all of that momentum into Sunday school and children's church?

1. Plan ahead. (Here's another item you can delegate.) Vacation Bible school will zap your energy, so it's important to have a plan in place well before VBS starts for how you'll follow up when it's over. What will your Sunday morning program be like? Be sure you have something just as dynamic and exciting waiting for kids who come back to try Sunday school.

2. Learn and use kids' names during VBS. Sounds simple, but this is often overlooked. Kids will flock to a place where they feel valued, accepted, and welcomed. Speaking a child's name in love is a powerful way to draw him or her back to your church. This is one reason it's important to use small, relationship-building groups in your VBS structure. Such groups foster more meaningful friendships. (Be sure to encourage your staff in this simple practice. It's a great way to demonstrate God's love.)

3. Be sure your children's ministry areas look inviting. Of course you'll have loads of thematic decorations, but don't hide the fact that this is a child-friendly facility year-round. Do your classrooms look like fun places to visit, or do they just look like school? Are there engaging posters of children on the walls or only "adult-looking" décor? A clean, bright, and inviting facility will be particularly welcoming to kids who have never been to church before.

4. Talk about Sunday school...a *lot*! From the first day of VBS, let kids know that this church has tons of fun ways to learn about God. Mention that you'll be singing these VBS songs in children's church. Tell kids that these are just *some* of the cool stories in the Bible. Sprinkle your conversations with countless mentions of the awesome ministry you have for kids.

5. Invite kids right away. Take advantage of a time kids are together on the last day of VBS (such as a closing program or rally). Let them know that the fun doesn't have to end today; in fact there's more excitement waiting on Sunday morning. As children leave, distribute colorful fliers with your church service times and other pertinent information.

6. And invite kids again! One week after vacation Bible school, mail a thank you letter to each child for attending. (Even better, make it a personal letter from the child's small group leader or teacher.) Let kids know that you're glad they came and that there are more fun ways to learn about God's love every week.

7. Connect with parents *during* VBS. Since most kids can't get to Sunday school without the help of a parent, it's crucial to draw parents in as well. Starting early in the week, take the time to introduce yourself to parents you don't know. Tell them your name, your role at the church, and how glad you are that their child has come to VBS. Let parents know of other youth, family, or children's ministry opportunities your church offers.

8. Have a photo opportunity. Few parents can resist the opportunity to film or photograph their children onstage doing just about anything. So plan a simple closing program or VBS worship time on a Friday night. Bring kids onstage to sing VBS songs, watch VBS skits, or tell what they liked about the program. Encourage kids to bring their parents, grandparents, and even neighbors.

9. Make the next connection a strong one. When a child *does* visit on Sunday morning, it's important that he or she sees familiar faces. Ask your leaders and teachers to be greeters for several Sundays following VBS. A warm welcome from someone who knows their child's name will speak volumes to visiting parents.

10. Consider planning a thematic VBS reunion. Yes, it's a bit more work, but it's a surefire way to bring kids back to church. A month after VBS ends, plan a simple reunion party. Send invitations to everyone on your registration lists. Decorate one room of your church with your VBS theme, play games, make crafts, sing songs, and eat snacks from VBS. Hold a slide show of the fun kids had at VBS. Distribute small autograph albums or T-shirts that kids can sign. And, of course, offer another invitation to your other child-friendly ministries!

Vacation Bible school is an important part of your children's ministry. It's an occasion to draw in church members who might not otherwise participate in children's ministry. It's an excuse to transform your church building into a circus or beach. And it's a wonderful opportunity to bring children into God's kingdom.

Vacation Bible School Registration Card

Child's name: _____

Child's address: _____

Home telephone: _____

Child's age: _____

Child's birth date: _____

In case of emergency, contact:_____

Emergency phone number: _____

Child's allergies: _____

Any medical information about the child we should know: _____

_____

---

twenty-one

Successful After-School and Midweek Programs

by Lori Owen Trousdale

Your children's ministry is a seven-days-per-week ministry, so why try to pack everything in on Sunday?

Adding a midweek or after-school program lets you reinforce what children learned on Sunday. You have opportunities to reach children who may never come on a weekend. And you can design programming that's targeted to meet the unique needs of your kids and your community.

In our Illinois community, we started an after-school program that gave children a safe place to play, do homework, and hang out. Within a few months, we were regularly influencing 10 percent of the elementary children in our entire town, including non-Christian kids.

And that certainly wouldn't have happened on a Sunday at 10:00 a.m.

Launching (or improving an existing) after-school or midweek program doesn't have to be a complicated process, but it does need to be an *organized* one. Here are some steps to consider...

After-School Programs

DETERMINE THE NEED

Determine the needs of your church, children, and community. If children don't need an after-school program, why have one? Ask parents, teachers, and others in your community what needs are not currently being met and how your church could minister to those needs. And remember that the other pastors and children's workers in your community can be your biggest resource.

FIND A FOCUS FOR YOUR AFTER-SCHOOL PROGRAM

Is this program a ministry or a community service? Is it outreach or designed to strengthen the kids already in your church? Answering these questions will help determine how your program is financed, who comes, who helps, and how your congregation receives the program.

If it's a service to community kids, the program won't be as overtly "Christian." Still, the program can benefit you as the host church. Kids get to know you and your volunteers. They get familiar with your facility. That makes it easier for kids to come back on a Sunday, so invite them!

If your after-school program is just for "your kids," then you'll want to be certain it connects to the rest of their Christian education. How will your Sunday school and after-school programming fit together?

And no matter what sort of after-school program you design, make sure you include all involved parties in the process: your pastor, your church leaders, the janitor, and the ladies who organize the church kitchen you plan to use. You must all share a common vision for what you're trying to accomplish and why it's worth the extra effort.

For this to truly be a ministry of the Lord, your program needs to minister to your children, your volunteers, and to you.

IF YOU CREATE A PROGRAM TO DO OUTREACH...

• Advertise through the school system and PTA.

• Recruit volunteers who love to share Jesus.

• Enlist appropriate volunteers from the ranks of your local high school youth group, the Rotary Club, Fellowship of Christian Athletes, and other service organizations for volunteers.

• Set a participant limit, and insist that all participants' parents fill out parent or guardian permission cards, as well as medical release forms.

• Make completing homework a priority. (Give kids a quiet, supervised homework room in which to work.)

• Provide a variety of structured activities that can be used as witnessing opportunities for your volunteers (puppets, music, choir, guitar lessons, arts and crafts, recreation, clowning, rubber stamping, photography, cooking classes, or whatever else your volunteers are able to teach and lead).

• Provide a thirty-minute unstructured snack time when the children first get off the school bus or arrive. This is very important! You will *always* lose if you forget to do this!

• If you have enough children to fill up a bus, ask your school system to transport the kids directly to your facility.

• Advertise and enforce a definite end time. Talk with pre-school directors in your area to find out how they deal with habitually late parents. They usually levy a financial fine, and it may be appropriate to match their policy. If you don't have a policy in place, you risk losing volunteers who are stuck waiting until parents show up.

• Use this block of time to hold rehearsals for children's worship teams, Christmas concert rehearsals, and even children's small group meetings. Doing this allows children whose parents won't bring them back in the evening an opportunity to be involved in some awesome Christian programming. (See the faith I have in your programs?)

IF YOU CREATE A PROGRAM TO SERVE THE COMMUNITY...

• Enlist the help of other churches. Ask for donations of snacks, for volunteers, and for supplies.

• Make sure you really *are* being a service. Grumpy workers, poor facilities, and chaos aren't going to win the admiration of your community.

• Enlist the help of other community organizations: the Rotary Club, the fire department, the fraternal order of whomever, the Daughters of the American Revolution quilting bee—anyone you think believes kids should have a safe, nurturing environment. But give each volunteer the same rigorous screening to ensure children's safety.

• Meet with leaders from each of the organizations involved, and delegate specific duties such as providing snacks, tutoring homework, organizing recreation, setting up and taking down chairs, and teaching specialty classes.

IF YOU CREATE A PROGRAM TO STRENGTHEN YOUR KIDS...

• Still include the thirty-minute snack and unstructured activity time if you want to get anything else done. Trust me on this.

• Determine *why* you want only your church kids involved.

Are you using this time to prepare for Sunday programming or choir rehearsals or to start a small group discipleship program? Are you doing evangelism training? After-school is a tremendous outreach opportunity; if you aren't using it as one, know why.

• Most likely you'll need to arrange for carpooling or make a number of church van trips to provide transportation from the schools. Line up volunteers!

AFTER-SCHOOL AFTERTHOUGHTS

• After school means about 2:30 p.m. to 6:00 p.m. That's a long time! You can't do it alone, so build a strong team of parents and volunteers.

• Be specific about the age group of children you'll accept. It's better to start with a narrow age group and expand when the funds and staff become available.

• Make *sure* your church is committed to this program. Ask for the pastor to support it from the pulpit. Post after-school art projects, grade improvement statistics, and thank you letters to the church where church members will see them. This can only help when Mrs. Clayton discovers an after-school child carved his initials on her Sunday school table.

• Discipline: It can be your best friend. Post a few clear rules where everyone can see them, and make sure everyone abides by them. Review the rules regularly and proactively, not just when someone breaks a rule. Your rules might include: Finish your homework first, place book bags in designated areas only, no running, keep snacks in snack area, no cussing, respect church property and each other, no one may go to the bathroom unless given permission, only two people in the bathroom at a time. Keep rules simple, crystal clear, and as few in number as possible.

• Remember that it's your job to keep things safe and equitable. If a child is unable or unwilling to abide by the rules, involve the child's parents and push for resolution. If necessary, suspend the child from the program for a period of time. Don't compromise the integrity of your program.

• Get donations from everyone, everywhere, in every form. Take snacks from the grocery stores and money from civic clubs. Become a member of the Rotary Club and take their money. Speak at every organization from which you can beg an invitation. Show them pictures of hardworking kids and report cards with A's on them, and then ask for money. Ask Sunday school classes and other adult groups within your congregation to supply craft supplies and snacks and sponsor different weeks of the program. An after-school program I started had a monthly budget of $1,200 that came entirely from one-time donations and community sponsors.

• Consider paying a few workers to be at the program daily. This guarantees you'll never be short-handed.

• Only start specialty classes when people are ready and willing to use their gifts to teach that class. For example, Miss Martha was the best cook in our church, so we waited for her to decide to help before we opened Miss Martha's Cooking Class. Pastor John played the guitar. It was only after he volunteered to teach that we opened up the guitar class.

• Know your students. Have a questionnaire filled out by each student, and use the information for follow-up visits to children's homes.

• Evaluate! Meet weekly with your paid staff and monthly with everyone else. Listen and act on suggestions. And before you jump to implement an outsider's suggestions, talk with your workers. Your volunteers know if something can be done or not.

While an after-school program may be a completely new venture for many churches, hosting a midweek program is often already a tradition. But is it an effective one? It pays to ask some hard questions.

Here's a sample of an after-school program form you'll want every child's parents or guardians to fill out:

Homework Hangout Enrollment Form and Medical Release

Child's name: _____ Age: _____ Grade: _____

Child's parents' names: _____

Child's home address: _____

Child's home phone: _____

Other address (if child does not live with both parents) _____

_____ Other phone: _____

Please list all allergies or other pertinent medical information:

Please list everyone who is allowed to pick up your child (NO children are allowed to walk home without written permission.):

Is your child currently involved in divorce proceedings or custody battle? _____

If yes, please explain any special needs pertaining to this: _____

_____

_____

I, _____, the custodial parent/guardian for

_____, give permission for him/her to attend the Homework Hangout on (please circle) Monday Tuesday Wednesday Thursday Friday. I understand that my child will receive the greatest care; however, in the event of an emergency, I authorize those working on behalf of Homework Hangout to seek and obtain medical care for my child.

Parent or Guardian Signature: _____

Date: _____

Here's a form you'll want every child to fill out:

Getting to Know You!

Name:_____Nickname:_____

Birthday:_____Age:_____Grade:_____

Address:_____

Phone:_____Emergency number:_____

Parents' names:_____

Fill in the blanks!

I live with (include pets too!)_____
_____.

My favorite movie is_____. The last movie I
saw at the movie theater was_____.
The last movie I saw on video was _____
_____.

My favorite song (right now) is_____.
My favorite music group (right now) is_____.

If you go home after school is anyone there?_____
Who?_____

What's something you want us to know about you?_____
_____

Midweek Programs

DETERMINE THE NEED

Does your midweek program run simultaneously with an adult program, or does it stand alone? Are you creating a new ministry or giving a shot of excitement to one that's fading fast? Do you already have volunteers, or will you need to start from scratch? These are all considerations, but the most important thing is to pick a midweek program that best meets your ministry goals. Among the programs available are…

• *High religious content*—If you value lots of memorization and cute little badges, consider Awana. But be mindful that there are restrictions about what your church must believe before you'll be allowed to host a club. Visit www.awana.org/StartGroup.asp for more details.

• *High relationship-building and faith-building content*—If you value small groups that encourage friendships and accountability and seeing kids apply their faith through child-sized service projects, FW Friends is a good pick. Visit www.fwfriends.com for more information.

• *High community involvement and environmental care*—If you value service projects, skill building, and learning to conserve and care for the earth, consider Cub Scouts (www.scouting.org /nav/signup.html) or Brownies (www.girlscouts.org/joinus.html).

• *High relationship-building and ministry content*—If you value plugging your kids into your church, create teams that meet specifically to prepare for weekend ministry like a children's choir, a puppet ministry team, or a Kids' Prayer Warriors team.

Any of these program ideas can be used to encourage your kids to invite friends.

FIND A FOCUS FOR MIDWEEK

Answer these questions to bring your program into focus:
- What does this program need to accomplish?
- Which children will this program serve?
- How does this program compliment our church's mission?
- What are the staffing and budget considerations?
- How will I know this program is successful?

As you and your church leadership answer these questions together, you'll narrow down your options and begin to lay the foundation for a midweek program that fits within the mission of your larger children's ministry. You'll identify which kids you want to serve and how. And you'll get a clear picture of what resources it's going to take to pull it all off.

THOUGHTS ABOUT MAKING MIDWEEK WORK

- Remember that children arrive at your midweek program with brains already fried from all the schoolwork they've done. You'll probably want to include way more celebration than study if you want kids to be involved and enthusiastic about attending.

- You don't have to reinvent the wheel by writing a special curriculum. You can find great lessons through existing, dated midweek curriculum (like FW Friends) or by using the second hour of lesson ideas found in most Sunday school dated curriculum. You can even take a great VBS program and use one lesson a week.

- Remember that there's no Saturday night in front of Wednesday. Most Sunday school lessons are prepared at the last possible moment by busy volunteers. They won't have a chance to cram for Wednesday night, so look for a curriculum resource that's both easy to prepare and easy for a substitute to pick up and use.

Ready to tackle your after-school program or midweek program? Well, almost. There's still one other thing to do: pray. Ask God's guidance as you make decisions that involve his children.

twenty-two

Special Ministries for Special Needs

by Pat Verbal

Two days before Christmas, the shocking headline read, "Parents Abandon Disabled Son."

Steven, a ten-year-old with cerebral palsy, was left at an emergency room with some of his toys, a file containing his medical records, and a note saying his parents could no longer care for him. These middle-class parents, who were charged with abandonment, had been unable to deal with the chronic stress that had built up over time.[1] How could a family become so frustrated in caring for their child that abandonment felt like their only option?

For years, church growth experts have challenged churches to find a need and meet it. But what about families faced with disabilities through birth defects, disease, or accidents? After twenty-five years in ministry, I've come to believe that these families represent one of the largest untapped mission fields in the church world today. The shocking fact is that they live, work, and struggle right next door to the church.

What support would Steven's family find at *your* church?

"None!" replies Leslie, a children's pastor at a growing church in Dallas. "I know our church needs to do something for children with special needs, but I don't have a clue where to start. I've read about the high divorce rate among couples who have children with disabilities, and it just breaks my heart," says Leslie sadly.

It takes a compassionate heart to start a special needs ministry, but these families don't need sympathy. They need to feel good about being at church.

Jesus Saw Those With Special Needs—Do You?

The "special need" you most need to deal with is the one that walks through the door of your church. You could spend months planning to meet every conceivable special needs situation that might arise, and all that frantic planning may keep you from taking the first, simple step.

That first step is to respond to the special needs God has already brought into your congregation.

At one church where I served, the special needs ministry was defined by several foster parents who brought infants on heart monitors to the nursery. In another church, it started with an exhausted mom and dad who brought two preschoolers with Down syndrome and one with autism. Look around your congregation. Do you see any families with special needs children? They're probably there, even if the needs aren't immediately obvious to you or others.

Special needs are disabilities that prevent children from progressing at the customary pace mentally, physically, or emotionally. While disabilities are extremely diverse, they often share common symptoms such as…

- hyperactivity with short attention span,
- distractibility and impulsiveness,
- poor visual/motor skills and large muscle and fine motor coordination,
- rapid and excessive changes of mood and reasoning,
- faulty perception with repetition of a thought or action, and/or
- problems with social interaction and inconsistent and unpredictable behavior.

Each child is unique. Each can know the love of Jesus. And families with special needs children have lessons to teach us. Handicaps have the power to draw families toward God's grace. Churches that reach out to these families and their children are promised a blessing in Luke 14:13-14a: "But when you give a banquet, invite the poor, the crippled, the lame, the blind, and you will be blessed."

Consider: Your church might need these children more than they need you.

Jesus Welcomed All Children—Do You?

When the National Council of Churches' Committee on Disabilities created a policy statement regarding special needs children, it rested on four foundational principles[2]:

1. All people are created in the image of God (Genesis 1:26). This image is not a measurable set of characteristics.

2. All people are called by God (Ephesians 2:10). When Jesus invited children to come to him, there's no evidence he added conditions that the children couldn't be on crutches or in wheelchairs,

be developmentally disabled, or be victims of abuse.

3. All people have special gifts (1 Corinthians 12:4). The gifts God has to give each person are needed by all other people, and no one is unnecessary.

4. All people are invited to participate in God's ministry (1 Corinthians 12:7). Yet we don't see many disabled people serving on the church board, singing in the choir, teaching classes, or greeting visitors at the front door.

The lack of people with handicaps serving in visible ways bothers Dr. James Dobson, founder of Focus on the Family: "People who have handicaps come [to church]…and see the absence of anybody else like themselves, and they feel a wall of misunderstanding and disapproval…I really feel that the Christian church is going to have to examine its values at this point, because there but for the grace of God go I or my child."[3]

Jesus Modeled Compassion — Do You?

Starting a special needs ministry is a good idea, even if you don't have any children with disabilities right now. You'll discover that these families come only after you've demonstrated a commitment to meeting the needs of their children. These families have already discovered that, sadly, the church isn't one of their most reliable helpers in working with their children.

With God's help, my friend Leslie determined to change that image and open the doors of her Dallas church to this exciting new ministry. She and I sat down over a long lunch to discuss six practical steps to starting a special needs ministry.

Getting Started: Six Practical Steps

STEP 1: BUILD AWARENESS

It has been said that all lack of evangelism is due to a lack of love. That may be true of evangelism, but the lack of special needs ministries is probably due more to a shortage of information.

Many adults are isolated from these great boys and girls who challenge all of us to be more like Jesus. Folks don't know what to say when a beautiful young couple announces that their newborn has spina bifida or is severely retarded—unless there is already an active special needs ministry at their church. In that case, lay people can offer hope from the testimonies of families who have trusted God to cope with their children's impairments.

Children also may not have experience dealing with disabilities in others.

Children snickered when six-year-old Robert left his seat at our children's church and wandered up on the stage to touch objects the leader was using to illustrate a point. Robert wore thick glasses and attended a special school for the blind.

One Sunday when Robert was absent, I asked the class if they understood what Robert's life was like. They didn't. We discussed it, and when I asked if Robert should continue to be a part of the class or instead attend a special class with a caring teacher, the children stared at me. "No way!" they said in unison. Robert was an important—and now understood—part of the class. He *had* to stay!

Building awareness in both adults and children opens doors of understanding. Among ways you can build awareness and empathy in your congregation are these:

• Invite guest speakers with disabilities to share in person or by video. *Blessings Out of Brokenness* is a four-part video series by Joni Tada that will minister to all ages.[4]

• Cover special needs families with love by placing a bright red umbrella in the church foyer. Decorate it with pictures, names, and addresses of several community families who care for children with disabilities. "Shower" these families with love by sending them encouraging notes and praying for them.

• Special Olympics is a dream come true for many families. These events boost self-esteem, promote healthy relationships, and provide fun for all participants. Many communities would like to host Special Olympics but lack volunteers. Challenge your church to support these community efforts by donating money and time.[5]

• Encourage church members to volunteer in area special needs schools and treatment centers. Your people will not only develop empathy, but they'll also receive valuable training.

STEP 2: ORGANIZE LEADERS

Jesus was a team builder. You need a team, too. Pray for a special needs director and four coordinators to lead a quality program.

The *special needs director* oversees policies and procedures, liability issues, facility needs, and budgets, and recruits and trains volunteers. This person also stays abreast of issues facing the disabled community.

The *prayer coordinator* prepares prayer guides for adult classes and support groups and keeps specific requests before the congregation.

The *publicity coordinator* provides displays and bulletin boards with informative brochures collected from special needs organizations, handles newsletters and brochures, and organizes an annual Special Needs Awareness Sunday.[6]

The *program coordinator* designs a special needs survey to determine the needs of the church family, researches programs available in the community, and plans social events and support groups.

One of our best events ever was an annual Royal Hearts Fifties

Party. Kids wore poodle skirts, bobby socks, and black leather jackets. They loved the Hula-Hoop contest and singing along to Elvis Presley recordings. Parents enjoyed a free night out, and volunteers talked about the fun for months.

The *classroom coordinator* creates registration forms for children and helps the director place children in classes with caregivers or in a special needs class. The classroom coordinator evaluates curriculum and recommends resources.

STEP 3: TRAIN YOUR CHURCH STAFF

When a family with a special needs child visits a church, they have one key question: "Will people accept us?" An usher's warm smile can set the tone for their whole day. Greeters and teachers of all ages should know the proper procedure for registering children. Senior pastors, with little or no special needs training in seminary, can grow right along with the staff.

Louise Tucker Jones, co-author of *Extraordinary Kids*, brags on her senior pastor's welcome of her son, Jay, who has Down syndrome: "Every Sunday morning, Jay would run to our pastor after the service ended. The pastor would scoop him up in his arms and hold him while shaking hands with church members. I offered more than once to take Jay, but the pastor refused. In doing this, not only did he show his own love for Jay, but he also allowed the church members to meet and love Jay in a special way."[7]

From the first-impression handshake of an usher to the sensitivity of the senior pastor, training matters. Be sure resources get into your church staff's hands—and minds.

And you needn't create all resources yourself. Following is a list of solid organizations that can provide a wealth of training booklets, study guides, forms, and videos.

Organizations to Contact for Training Materials:

Joni and Friends Ministries
(818) 707-5664
www.joniandfriends.org

American Speech-Language-Hearing
Association
1-800-638-8255
www.asha.org

Children and Adults with Attention-
Deficit/Hyperactivity Disorder
1-800-233-4050
www.chadd.org

Cystic Fibrosis Foundation
1-800-344-4823
www.cff.org

Parents Helping Parents
(408) 727-5775
www.php.com

Independent Living Research Utilization
(713) 520-0232
www.ilru.org

Muscular Dystrophy Association
1-800-572-1717
www.mdausa.org

National Information Center for
Children and Youth with Disabilities
1-800-695-0285
www.nichcy.org

Spina Bifida Association of America
1-800-621-3141
www.sbaa.org

United Cerebral Palsy Association
1-800-872-5827
www.ucpa.org

STEP 4: ESTABLISH PROCEDURES

Clear procedures give your ministry a clear direction. Help volunteers feel secure in their roles. Let parents know what to expect. And clear procedures let you make decisions about how to handle difficult decisions *before* they actually occur.

Be sure you establish procedures in the following areas:

What training is required? In addition to the usual children's ministry volunteer screening, you may wish to require additional training. Decide that now, and make no exceptions.

What's your position regarding leader/child ratios? Ask yourself what level of care you wish to provide. What do your kids deserve?

What's your approach to ministering to children? My friend Leslie faced a challenge when the protective parents of a thirteen-year-old mentally disabled girl insisted on keeping her with them in the adult class. Class members sympathized but felt the girl was disruptive. A showdown was averted—and effective ministry provided—because Leslie had already decided to use a buddy system for children like the girl.

In a buddy system, children are mainstreamed into their age-appropriate classes. A buddy (caregiver or friend) is assigned to one student and gets to know him or her by visiting with parents and teachers. The buddy becomes a role model who helps the student succeed in class and at other social events. Some buddies prefer to work in teams where they serve on a rotation schedule.

Another approach might be reverse mainstreaming, where classmates join a special needs class to interact and minister. Combining these two plans allows children to join peers for part of the time and still enjoy their own class if they get tired or the group activity is too stimulating.

Having a policy already in place made it easy for Leslie to help the girl's parents release their daughter in a well-organized ministry that met her needs.

How will you handle discipline? Knowing what is and isn't appropriate discipline is hugely helpful to volunteers. Incorporate the following information into your training and procedures.

> ## Discipline Do's and Don'ts
> ## With Special Needs Children
>
> Children who face handicaps every day may be hyperactive, shy, aggressive, defeated, tired, or antagonistic. Some are on medication that may alter their moods.
>
> So don't...
> - expect perfect behavior,
> - allow a child to take control of your classroom,
> - create too many rules,
> - try to succeed without help from parents and caregivers.
>
> And do...
> - recognize the need for individual attention;
> - create situations in which the child can succeed;
> - acknowledge a child's feelings, especially negative ones;
> - be sure the children know you're on their side.

When faced with new experiences, these children may fear failure and say, "I can't." Acknowledge that something might be hard for them, but assure them you'll be there to help.

STEP 5: EVALUATE YOUR FACILITIES AND CURRICULUM RESOURCES

Leslie's church met building codes to provide physical access to people with limitations, and her Sunday morning classrooms were full. Yet there were more opportunities to make a positive difference in the lives of families throughout the week.

"Respite Care" programs—programs that give caregivers a brief rest—are popular because they provide free child care once or twice a month on a Friday night. Parents can go out to dinner, shop, or just relax at home while loving caregivers play with their children.

"I see this as evangelism," says Donna, a Respite Care director. "So many families are staying home from church. We need to be 'Jesus with skin on.' I just want to see all these people saved."

When selecting or adapting curriculum resources, be sure your children have experiences that let them enjoy being at church and help them feel successful. And use resources that let your volunteers feel competent and relaxed.

Children with physical or emotional handicaps can use regular, age-appropriate lessons but usually move through lessons at a slower pace. For those with mental impairments, select themes and vocabulary that match their developmental levels. Older children need art and music that doesn't seem babyish. Ask the following questions concerning your curriculum choice.

> *For a comprehensive list of facility requirements and concerns, contact the National Organization on Disability at 910 16th St. N.W., Suite 600, Washington, DC 20006.*

- Is it learner-based and appealing to different learning styles?
- Will it work well in small groups with individualized instruction?
- Is it simple, teaching one principle at a time?
- Are the activities physically adaptable to accommodate children in wheelchairs and children who have other physical restrictions?
- Is it fun? Are there puppets, games, skits, cooking activities, and arts and crafts? Most children with special needs will try anything and enjoy your class so much that they won't want to leave.

STEP 6: REACH OUT TO PARENTS

Realize that you're ministering to entire families. Parents and grandparents need support groups. Pray with family members, and listen to their concerns. Rejoice with them in the victories. Offer hope for their child's future.

Jesus Has a Plan

My final advice to Leslie (and you) is to watch for what God wants to do in *your* life as you become involved with a special needs ministry.

My passion for investing in these children began in 1990 when I became children's pastor at a church with a growing special needs ministry. When their regular teachers were absent, my husband, Dick, and I gladly substituted. Two years later, a precious little girl with Down syndrome became a part of our family. Jessica won our hearts immediately, and Jesus used her to deepen our faith in his sovereignty.

Did you ever think that perhaps *we're* the ones with a "special need"?

Endnotes

1. Aaron Krach, *When Stress Overwhelms Disabled Kids' Parents*, www.cbshealthwatch.com/cx/viewarticles/211808.

2. National Council of Churches Web site at www.nccusa.org

3. Cheri Fuller and Louise Tucker Jones, *Extraordinary Kids*, (Colorado Springs, CO: Focus on the Family, 1997), 234.

4. Joni Tada, *Blessings Out of Brokenness*, 4 videos, 45 minutes each, (818) 523-5777.

5. Special Olympics, Inc., (202) 628-3630, www.specialolympics .org

6. See Joni and Friends at www.joniandfriends.org for a resource packet.

7. Fuller and Jones, *Extraordinary Kids*, 225.

contributors

JODY BROLSMA is part of the award-winning team of authors that created *Group's Hands-On Bible Curriculum* and is the Senior Editor of Group's Vacation Bible School program. She's an active children's ministry volunteer at her church in Colorado.

JEAN COZBY has served as a director of nurseries in Washington and has worked with children for more than twenty years.

MARY IRENE FLANAGAN, C.S.J. is the author of *Preschool Handbook, Me at Three*, and *Me at Four* as well as other books. She is serving in Manhattan Beach, California.

LISA FLINN is a former public school teacher and the author of *Meditations to Make Teachers Smile*, and she has worked with children for twenty-two years.

BEN F. FREUDENBURG is author of *The Family Friendly Church* (with Rick Lawrence) and serves as a Minister to the Christian Home in Phoenix, Arizona.

MARY RICE HOPKINS is a Christian musician whose busy concert schedule includes special shows for children and families. Visit Mary at www.maryricehopkins.com for more information.

VINCE ISNER is a writer, director, and producer, and he has hosted his own children's television program. He has worked with children for more than twenty years.

CRAIG JUTILA author of *Leadership Essentials for Children's Ministry*, leads twenty-four paid staff, eight hundred volunteer leaders, and three thousand children at Saddleback Church, one of the largest churches in America. He's also a husband and dad.

SUE MILLER is the Executive Director of Promiseland, the children's ministry at Willow Creek Community Church in Barrington, Illinois. Her responsibilities include leading and directing a ministry that reaches three thousand children and one thousand adult volunteers each weekend. Before coming to Promiseland, Sue taught for fifteen years in the public school system.

BETH ROWLAND helped develop and shape Group's *KidsOwn Worship* program and is active in ministry through her local church.

THOM AND JOANI SCHULTZ are the authors of *The Dirt on Learning* and several other books. Thom is the president of Group Publishing and Joani is Group's chief creative officer. Both have local church ministry experience.

MIKE SCIARRA has over sixteen years of local church ministry experience and is the pastor of adults and families at Voyagers Bible Church in Irvine, California.

BILL STOUT is co-author of *The Good Shepherd Program*, a resource for churches wanting to encourage child safety in their ministries.

RaNae Street is the Children's Ministry Director at Ginghamsburg Church in Tipp City, Ohio. RaNae has over fifteen years of experience working with children and is a frequent workshop leader.

Mary Gray Swan has served as a director of Christian education and has published denominational church curriculum for children.

Lori Owen Trousdale has launched successful after-school programs at both large and small churches and has authored children's lessons published by Group's *FW Friends* preschool program.

Pat Verbal is a frequent workshop leader and children's ministry consultant and author of *My Family's Prayer Calendar 2002* (with Shirley Dobson) as well as other family resources.

Terry Vermillion is a former director of a preschool program in Missouri. She has contributed to several books.

Dale and Liz VonSeggen are the authors of *Puppet Ministry Made Easy* and dozens of other puppet resources. Dale is founder and president of One Way Street, Inc., where Liz is director of new products.

Gordon and Becki West are popular conference presenters on many topics, including preteen ministry. They're founders and co-directors of Kids at Heart, a Christian-education consulting ministry based in Mesa, Arizona.

Dan Wiard has worked in ministry for twenty years and serves as director of Christian education in Virginia Beach, Virginia.

Jim Wideman has worked in children's ministry since 1978 and is currently the children's pastor and the director of Christian education at Church on the Move in Tulsa, Oklahoma, where he oversees ministries that minister to over 4,500 children weekly.

Barbara Younger is author of *Purple Mountain Majesties: The Story of Katherine Lee Bates and "America the Beautiful"* and has twenty-five years of Christian education experience.

Christine Yount is executive editor of Children's Ministry Magazine and the national Children's Ministry Magazine Live workshops.

Group Publishing, Inc.
Attention: Product Development
P.O. Box 481
Loveland, CO 80539
Fax: (970) 679-4370

Evaluation for
Children's Ministry That Works!

Please help Group Publishing, Inc. continue to provide innovative and useful resources for ministry. Please take a moment to fill out this evaluation and mail or fax it to us. Thanks!

● ● ●

1. As a whole, this book has been (circle one)

not very helpful   very helpful

1   2   3   4   5   6   7   8   9   10

2. The best things about this book:

3. Ways this book could be improved:

4. Things I will change because of this book:

5. Other books I'd like to see Group publish in the future:

6. Would you be interested in field-testing future Group products and giving us your feedback? If so, please fill in the information below:

Name_____

Church Name _____

Denomination _____ Church Size _____

Church Address _____

City _____ State _____ ZIP _____

Church Phone _____

mail _____

**If *Children's Ministry That Works!*
was helpful, dive even deeper with...**

Leadership Essentials
for Children's Ministry
by Craig Jutila

Craig Jutila and his team have built a cutting-edge children's ministry that's touching thousands of lives each week at Saddleback Church in California. In this book, Craig shares insights that will give you and your team powerful leadership skills as you focus on four critical foundational principles:

PASSION—It's essential to approach ministry as an energizing act of worship, not a chore.

ATTITUDE—Our mind-set determines our level of happiness and satisfaction within our ministry.

TEAMWORK—Succeeding in leadership requires us to link up with people whose gifts support and complement our own.

HONOR—To enjoy a growing ministry we must serve in an atmosphere of mutual respect and encouragement.

In *Leadership Essentials for Children's Ministry,* you'll learn from the practical experience of a top children's ministry leader how to build (or rebuild) a dynamic children's ministry in your church.

ISBN 0-7644-2389-4